OXFORD REVISION GUIDES

GCSE

PHYSICS
through diagrams

Brian Arnold

Oxford University Press

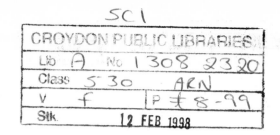
Oxford University Press,
Great Clarendon Street, Oxford OX2 6DP

Oxford New York
Athens Auckland Bangkok Bogota Bombay
Buenos Aires Calcutta Cape Town Dar es Salaam
Delhi Florence Hong Kong Istanbul Karachi
Kuala Lumpur Madras Madrid Melbourne
Mexico City Nairobi Paris Singapore
Taipei Tokyo Toronto Warsaw

and associated companies in
Berlin Ibadan

Oxford is a trade mark of Oxford University Press

© **Brian Arnold**

First published 1997 as Revise Through Diagrams - Physics
Revised and enlarged New Edition published 1997

School edition   ISBN 0 19 914713 2
Bookshop edition ISBN 0 19 914714 0

A CIP catalogue record for this book is available from the
British Library.

Acknowledgements:
We are grateful to the following Examination Boards for permission to use GCSE examinations questions and specimen
questions (Sp = specimen):

Questions (including all multiple choice questions) have been provided by **London Examinations**, a division of Edexcel
Foundation. Edexcel Foundation, London Examinations accepts no responsibility whatsoever for the accuracy or method
of working in the answers given. **MEG**: questions from MEG reproduced by kind permission of the Midland Examining
Group. The Midland Examining Group bears no responsibility for the example answers to questions taken from its past
question papers which are contained in this publication. **NICCEA**: questions from NICCEA are reproduced with the
permission of the Northern Ireland Council for the Curriculum, Examinations and Assessment. The Northern Ireland
Council for the Curriculum, Examinations and Assessment bears no responsibility for the example answers to questions
taken from its past question papers which are contained in this publication. **SEG**: questions from SEG are reproduced
with the kind permission of the Southern Examining Group. The Southern Examining Group bears no responsibility for
the example answers to questions taken from its past question papers which are contained in this publication. **WJEC**:
questions from WJEC are reproduced with the kind permission of the Welsh Joint Education Committee. The Welsh
Joint Education Committee bears no responsibility for the example answers to questions taken from its past question
papers which are contained in this publication.

All answers are the responsibility of the author.

Typeset and illustrated by Hardlines, Charlbury, Oxford
Printed and bound in Great Britain

CONTENTS

How to use this book

This book is arranged into three main sections:
SECTION 1: EXAMINATIONS AND REVISION
SECTION 2: SUBJECT CONTENT
SECTION 3: QUESTIONS

USING SECTION 1: EXAMINATIONS AND REVISION

- Read the **GCSE PHYSICS EXAMINATIONS** table to identify:
  your examination
  how it is examined
  the types of examination papers
  the styles of questions

- Work out a revision programme using the **REVISION TIMETABLE** and place copies around your home.

- Use the **REVISION PATHWAYS** to help you navigate easily through your planned revision programme.

- Read **HOW TO REVISE** for some general guidelines on successful revision techniques.

- Remind yourself how to answer questions by reading the **MODEL ANSWERS**.

USING SECTION 2: SUBJECT CONTENT

- Use a copy of your syllabus to identify those pages you need to revise as part of your revision programme.

- Mark your revision pages on the **CHECKLISTS** and on the **REVISION PATHWAYS** with a highlighter pen.

- Each time you revise a page tick it off on the **CHECKLISTS/PATHWAYS**.

- Use highlighter pens to identify key words and concepts on individual pages.

- Colour in parts of the diagrams to help you to remember them more easily.

- Use pages from this book to test yourself with a friend.

USING SECTION 3: QUESTIONS

- With this section you can:
  follow your progress
  build your confidence in answering questions
  identify your strengths and weaknesses
  choose questions from the *Foundation* or *Higher* tiers

Variety and styles of examination question

The examination papers set by the different examination groups are likely to contain three styles of questions: **Multiple choice**; **Short answers/Structured questions**; **Free response/Long questions**.

MULTIPLE CHOICE QUESTIONS

This type of question is usually done on a special Multiple Choice answer form which is computer marked.

Even if your particular examination does not include Multiple Choice questions they provide useful examination level questions to work through. They also help you to focus on small sections of the syllabus. Also they are useful to help identify areas of weakness or confusion.

Each question gives you four (or some examinations: five) alternatives. Only one is correct. Your task is to select the correct one.

how to answer them

- *CHOOSE ONLY ONE ANSWER*: Select just one answer for each question – if more than one has been selected the question will be marked wrong.

- *WATCH THE TIME*: Keep an eye on the clock. You will be able to answer some questions immediately you have finished reading them, others may take several minutes to work out. Nevertheless, as a rough guide check that halfway through the examination you are approximately halfway through the paper.

- *ELIMINATE INCORRECT ANSWERS*: If the correct answer isn't obvious then eliminate those answers you know to be incorrect. Select an answer. Then mark the question on your question sheet with a star or asterisk so that you can identify it as a question to return to towards the end of the examination.

- *ANSWER ALL THE QUESTIONS*: At the end of the examination don't leave any multiple choice questions unanswered – if all else fails guess!

Before filling in the form you should know:

- how to indicate which answer you have selected

- what to do if you want to change your answer

All this is explained on the form itself but you may feel happier if you have already seen one or used one prior to the exam itself. Your teacher will almost certainly have some examples from previous years that you can have a look at.

Typical example:

1. Which of the following types of radiation is NOT part of the electromagnetic spectrum?
   A infrared radiation
   B ultraviolet radiation
   C sound waves
   D radio waves

MULTIPLE CHOICE ANSWER GRID

1. A ☐   B ☐   C ⬛   D ☐
2. A ☐   B ☐   C ☐   D ☐
3. A ⬛   B ☐   C ☐   D ☐
4. A ☐   B ⬛   C ☐   D ☐

HINT: Check carefully the types of examination questions you will have to answer

SHORT ANSWER/STRUCTURED QUESTIONS

This type of question is usually completed on the exam paper itself. Extended, wordy answers are not wanted here. Answers should be short, concise and complete (You may need answers from early parts of the question later on.)

Typical example:

1. The radioactive isotope carbon-14($^{14}_{6}$C) is used for carbon dating. It has a half life of 5730 years.

   (a) What is an isotope?

   ....

   ....

   (2 marks)

   (b) What is meant by the phrase 'half life of 5730 years'

   ....

   ....

   (2 marks)

How to answer them

- *ANSWER THE QUESTION*: if the question says state, then don't explain. If it says calculate, then show the calculation, don't just write the answer. Answer the question the way it asks to be answered.

- *GIVE FULL ANSWERS*: Give answers as fully as you can in the space provided. As a general rule if an answer is worth two marks there should be two pieces of information in your answer. If there are three or four lines provided for the answer then a one-word answer is unlikely to be sufficient.

- *SHOW ALL YOUR WORKING*: You have worked hard to revise so show the examiner how you arrive at your answers. Show all your working out; write down equations in symbols; substitute in your values and then work out your final answers. The working out is often worth more than the answer itself.

- *TIME YOURSELF*: Well before the exam, work out approximately how much time there is per mark on the paper. If the paper is 1 hour long and there are 120 marks available then 1 minute is equivalent to 2 marks. Use this as a guide to how much time you should spend on each question or part question.

- *TAKE YOUR TIME*: Be aware if you are on time-target or not, and don't panic. Remember, it is often much better to answer many questions partly than to fully answer only a few.

- *CHECK YOUR ANSWERS*: When you think you have finished and completed as much of the paper as you can stop and collect your thoughts. Now, read your answers again carefully to confirm that there are no omissions and that you really have written what you wanted to.

FREE RESPONSE/LONG QUESTIONS

This type of question is less common than it used to be but there are some papers where this style is still used.

These types of questions require extended answers. You must judge how much or how little is required. A good exam technique is particularly important here if you are to gain the maximum number of marks.

Typical example:

1. Explain the advantages and disadvantages of using renewable sources of energy, such as wind energy. Compare these advantages and disadvantages with those of using non-renewable sources of energy such as coal. (7 marks)

How to answer them

In addition to those suggestions given for Short Answer /Structured Questions:

- *KNOW WHAT IS REQUIRED*: Read the question carefully to ensure that you know precisely what the question is looking for. Incorrect interpretations with this type of question can mean losing a lot of marks.

- *PLAN YOUR ANSWER*: Sketch a plan of attack before tackling the question properly: will making some notes help you set out the answer more logically; are diagrams going to be useful? But, this is not an art exam so don't make diagrams too elaborate – and remember labels.

- *BE especially AWARE OF THE TIME*: Longer questions take much more time and effort to correct if you stray off your time-target.

COURSEWORK

The four skill areas that will be assessed through coursework are:

1 **Your ability to plan an experiment**

   - Can you plan a fair/safe practical procedure using the appropriate apparatus?

   - Can you predict the outcome of your experiment based on scientific knowledge?

2 **Your ability to obtain evidence (the accuracy of your observations and/or measurements)**

   - Can you use the appropriate apparatus to make accurate measurements or observations?

   - Can you record clearly and accurately your observations and measurements?

3 **Your ability to analyse your evidence and to draw conclusions from it.**

   - Can you construct appropriate diagrams, charts, graphs – to process your data?

   - Can you draw conclusions from your results and then link these with other scientific knowledge and your prediction?

4 **Your ability to evaluate your evidence**

   - Can you recognise measurements and observations that don't fit a pattern or that might be 'faulty'?

   - Can you explain why they arose and suggest changes in your experiment to improve the reliability of your observations or extend your enquiry.

As part of your course your teacher will assess your experimental and investigative skills. You will have many opportunities throughout your course to practise and improve these skills. Your teacher will tell you when the skills are to be tested and will make clear what proof you need to provide to demonstrate the level of your expertise.

Coursework very often has deadlines to achieve throughout the course. It may not be possible to hand work in late and be credited with marks towards your final examination. Check with your teacher.

NOTE: There are marks available for accurate spelling, punctuation, and grammar. Be sure to bear this in mind when you provide any written work.

**A final thought – examiners want you to do well.
By setting out your answers in a clear, complete and logical fashion you will help them to help you.**

GCSE Physics Examinations

EXAM GROUP/ SYLLABUS	TIER/ GRADES	PAPERS	time weighting%		QUESTION STYLES
EDEXCEL PHYSICS (1046)	FOUNDATION G-G	PAPER 1F	$(1\frac{1}{2}h)$	50%	Structured questions
		PAPER 2F	$(1h)$	25%	Structured questions
		COURSEWORK		25%	
	HIGHER D-A*	PAPER 3H	$(1\frac{1}{2}h)$	50%	Structured questions
		PAPER 4H	$(1h)$	25%	Structured questions
		COURSEWORK		25%	
MEG PHYSICS (1782)	FOUNDATION G-C	PAPER 1	$(1\frac{1}{2}h)$	50%	Structured questions
		PAPER 3	$(1\frac{1}{2}h)$	25%	Structured questions
		COURSEWORK		25%	
	HIGHER D-A*	PAPER 2	$(1\frac{1}{2}h)$	50%	Structured questions
		PAPER 4	$(1\frac{1}{2}h)$	25%	Structured questions
		COURSEWORK		25%	
NUFFIELD PHYSICS (1787)	FOUNDATION G-C	PAPER 1	$(1\frac{1}{2}h)$	50%	Structured questions
		PAPER 3	$(\frac{3}{4}h)$	25%	Structured questions
		COURSEWORK		25%	
	HIGHER D-A*	PAPER 2	$(1\frac{3}{4}h)$	50%	Structured questions
		PAPER 4	$(1h)$	25%	Structured questions
		COURSEWORK		25%	
NEAB PHYSICS (1181)	FOUNDATION G-C	PAPER 1	$(2h)$	75%	Structured questions
		COURSEWORK		25%	
	HIGHER D-A*	PAPER 1	$(2\frac{1}{4}h)$	75%	Structured questions
		COURSEWORK		25%	

EXAM GROUP/ SYLLABUS	TIER/ GRADES	PAPERS	time weighting%		QUESTION STYLES
NICCEA PHYSICS	FOUNDATION G-C	PAPER 1	$(1h)$	30%	Multiple choice and Structured questions
		PAPER 2	$(1\frac{1}{2}h)$	45%	Structured questions
		COURSEWORK		25%	
	HIGHER D-A*	PAPER 1	$(1\frac{1}{2}h)$	37.5%	Structured questions
		PAPER 2	$(1h)$	35.5%	Structured and free response questions
		COURSEWORK		25%	
SEG PHYSICS (2670)	FOUNDATION G-C	PAPER 1	$(1\frac{1}{2}h)$	50%	Structured and free response questions
		PAPER 3	$(1h)$	25%	
		COURSEWORK		25%	
	HIGHER D-A*	PAPER 4	$(1\frac{1}{2}h)$	50%	Structured and free response questions
		PAPER 5	$(1h)$	25%	
		COURSEWORK		25%	
WJEC PHYSICS (1782)	FOUNDATION G-C	PAPER 1	$(1\frac{1}{2}h)$	50%	Structured questions
		PAPER 3	$(1\frac{1}{2}h)$	25%	Structured questions
		COURSEWORK		25%	
	HIGHER D-A*	PAPER 2	$(1\frac{1}{2}h)$	50%	Structured questions
		PAPER 4	$(1\frac{1}{2}h)$	25%	Structured questions
		COURSEWORK		25%	

HINT: Use a highlighter pen to identify your examination papers

EXAMINATION GROUPS

EDEXCEL
London Examinations
Stewart House
32 Russell Square
London WC1B 5DN

MIDLAND EXAMINING GROUP (MEG)
Syndicate Buildings
1 Hills Road
Cambridge CB1 2EU

NORTHERN EXAMINATIONS AND ASSESSMENT BOARD (NEAB)
31-33 Springfield Avenue
Harrogate
North Yorkshire HG1 2HW

NORTHERN IRELAND COUNCIL FOR THE CURRICULUM, EXAMINATIONS AND ASSESSMENT (NICCEA)
Beechill House
42 Beechill Road
Belfast BT8 4RS

SOUTHERN EXAMINING GROUP (SEG)
Stag Hill House
Guildford
Surrey GU2 5XJ

WELSH JOINT EDUCATION COMMITTEE (WJEC)
245 Western Avenue
Cardiff CF5 2YX

Model answers

Knowing the correct answer to a question is often not enough to get you full marks in an examination. To demonstrate to an examiner the full extent of your ability and understanding you must show how you arrived at your answer.

It is important to remember that an examiner is trying to give you as many marks as possible. The way in which examination papers are worded and set out can give you valuable clues to obtaining maximum marks.

Typical example:

1. Write down two differences between the properties of alpha radiation and gamma radiation.

(2 marks)

TYPICAL ANSWERS:

Answer A:

Alpha radiation is affected by magnetic fields. Gamma radiation is unaffected by magnetic fields.

Gamma radiation is highly penetrating. Alpha radiation has a low penetrating power.

Comment: This answer will receive full marks as the candidate has done what the question asked. He/she has given two differences.

Answer B:

Alpha radiation is affected by magnetic fields.

Gamma radiation is highly penetrating.

Comment: This answer may receive no marks as the candidate has not fully answered the question. He/she has not given differences between the properties of the two radiations.

NOTE: The question asks for two differences and there are two marks to be awarded. It is likely that one mark will be awarded for each difference. Do not leave the answer blank if you only know one, you may still gain one mark for one difference.

Typical example:

2. Calculate the pd across the ends of a 33 Ω resistor when a current of 0.2 A passes through it.

....

....

....(3 marks)

TYPICAL ANSWERS:

Answer A:

Using $V = 1 \times R$ ✓

$V = 0.2 \times 33$ ✓

$V = 4.6$ volts ✗

Comment: This candidate has shown that he/she understands the science of this question even though the final answer is incorrect. He/she is likely to be awarded two of the three marks for stating the equation correctly and for inserting the values correctly.

Answer B:

6.6V

Comment: This candidate is likely to receive full marks – for the correct answer only. But had the answer been wrong no marks would have been given although the candidate might have understood fully the material being tested.

NOTE: In extended length questions it is quite possible you will need answers from earlier parts of the question to help you complete later parts of the question.

Answer C:

Using $V = 1 \times R$

$V = 0.2 \times 33$

$V = 6.6$ volts

Comment: This answer is certain to be awarded all three marks. It demonstrates clearly how the candidate has arrived at his or her answer.

NOTE: The question has provided three lines in which to answer the question. Use this 'space' information as a guide to the amount of space likely to be needed for the answer- in this case 3 lines, and the equation needed three lines to complete. Examination papers are set out with space to answer questions in the way the examiner wants the answer presented: in order to help you gain maximum marks!

Also, the question says 'Calculate' and not 'State' the answer – so you need to show the calculation.

How to revise

There is no one method of revising which works for everyone. It is therefore important to discover the approach that suits you best. The following rules may serve as general guidelines.

GIVE YOURSELF PLENTY OF TIME

Leaving your revision until the last minute reduces your changes of success. There are very few people who can revise everything 'the night before' and still do well in an examination the next day. You need to plan your revision timetable for some weeks before the examinations start.

PLAN YOUR REVISION TIMETABLE

Plan your revision timetable well before the examinations start. Once you have done this, follow it – don't be sidetracked. Stick your timetable somewhere prominent where you will keep seeing it – or better still put several around your home!!!!

RELAX

You will be working very hard revising. It is as important to give yourself some free time to relax as it is to work. So, build some leisure time into your revision timetable.

ASK OTHERS

Friends, relatives, teachers will be happy to help if you ask them. Go and talk to them if you are having any difficulties – don't just give up on something that is causing you a problem. And don't forget your parents too!

FIND A QUIET CORNER

Find the conditions in which you can revise most efficiently. Many people think they can revise in a noisy, busy atmosphere – most cannot! And don't try and revise in front of the television – it doesn't generally work. Revision in a distracting environment is very inefficient.

LET THE CHECKLISTS/PATHWAYS HELP YOU

Use the Checklists and Pathways. When you have completed a topic, mark it off. You can also mark off topics you already feel confident about. That way you won't waste time revising unnecessarily.

MAKE SHORT NOTES, USE COLOURS...

As you read through your work or your textbooks make brief notes of the key ideas and facts as you go along. But be sure to concentrate on understanding the ideas rather than just memorizing the facts. Use colours and highlighters to help you.

PRACTISE ANSWERING QUESTIONS

As you finish revising each topic try answering some questions. At first you may need to refer to your notes or textbooks. As you gain confidence you will be able to attempt questions unaided, just as you will in the exam.

GIVE YOURSELF A BREAK

When you are working, work for perhaps an hour then reward yourself with a short break for 15 to 20 minutes while you have a coffee or cola ... then go back for another period of revision.

Revision pathways

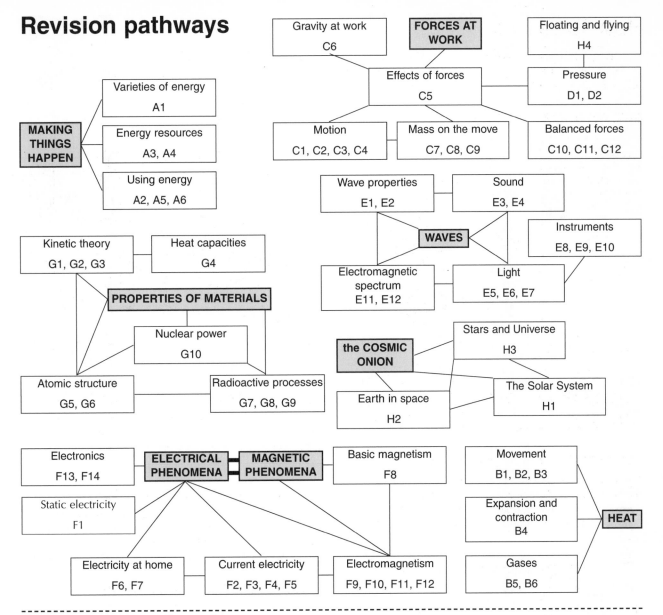

Gravity at work
C6

FORCES AT WORK

Floating and flying
H4

Effects of forces
C5

Pressure
D1, D2

MAKING THINGS HAPPEN

Varieties of energy
A1

Energy resources
A3, A4

Using energy
A2, A5, A6

Motion
C1, C2, C3, C4

Mass on the move
C7, C8, C9

Balanced forces
C10, C11, C12

Wave properties
E1, E2

Sound
E3, E4

WAVES

Instruments
E8, E9, E10

Kinetic theory
G1, G2, G3

Heat capacities
G4

Electromagnetic spectrum
E11, E12

Light
E5, E6, E7

PROPERTIES OF MATERIALS

Nuclear power
G10

the COSMIC ONION

Stars and Universe
H3

Atomic structure
G5, G6

Radioactive processes
G7, G8, G9

Earth in space
H2

The Solar System
H1

Electronics
F13, F14

ELECTRICAL PHENOMENA

MAGNETIC PHENOMENA

Basic magnetism
F8

Movement
B1, B2, B3

Static electricity
F1

Expansion and contraction
B4

HEAT

Electricity at home
F6, F7

Current electricity
F2, F3, F4, F5

Electromagnetism
F9, F10, F11, F12

Gases
B5, B6

Construct your own pathways here:

Revision Timetable

Subject: ....
Week beginning: ....
Week no: .... Exam in: .... weeks!

	Monday	Tuesday	Wednesday	Thursday	Friday	Saturday	Sunday	notes
morning								
afternoon								
evening (don't work too late!)								

End of day check: more work needed on?

1. ....
2. ....
3. ....

Timetable check: extra topics for next week?

1. ....
2. ....
3. ....

A1 Energy (1)

You need **energy** to live, to grow and to do things. Energy makes things happen. Anything which is able to do work is said to **possess** energy. Someone who is capable of doing lots of work is **energetic**. There are many different forms and sources of energy.

DIFFERENT FORMS OF ENERGY

Objects may have energy because of their position. This is called **gravitational potential energy**. Stone 1 has less potential energy. But stone 2, high above the beach has gravitational potential energy and so can ....

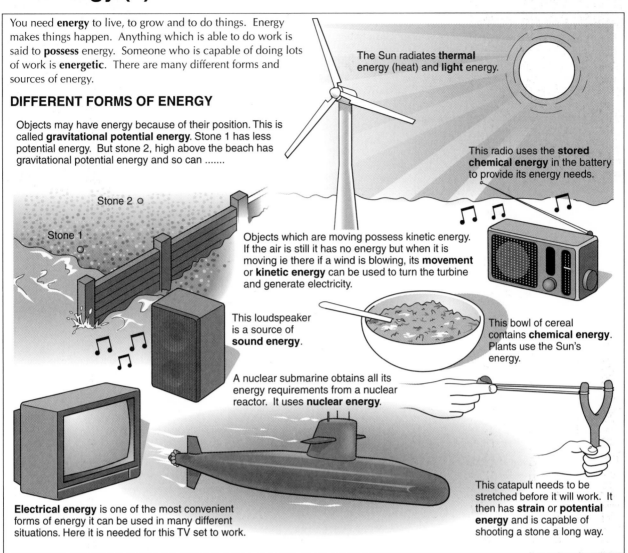

The Sun radiates **thermal** energy (heat) and **light** energy.

This radio uses the **stored chemical energy** in the battery to provide its energy needs.

Objects which are moving possess kinetic energy. If the air is still it has no energy but when it is moving ie there if a wind is blowing, its **movement** or **kinetic energy** can be used to turn the turbine and generate electricity.

This loudspeaker is a source of **sound energy**.

This bowl of cereal contains **chemical energy**. Plants use the Sun's energy.

A nuclear submarine obtains all its energy requirements from a nuclear reactor. It uses **nuclear energy**.

This catapult needs to be stretched before it will work. It then has **strain** or **potential energy** and is capable of shooting a stone a long way.

Electrical energy is one of the most convenient forms of energy it can be used in many different situations. Here it is needed for this TV set to work.

ENERGY TRANSFERS

When energy is converted it is transferred into a new form and work is done.

electrical energy in → heat and light energy out

This light bulb is doing work as it converts electrical energy into heat and light energy.

Energy is measured in **joules** (J). The number of joules of energy before and after a change is the same ie no energy is lost or gained. This is the **law of the conservation of energy**. The work done by the above light bulb can be represented by this (Sankey) diagram.

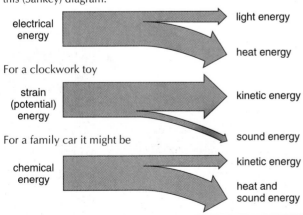

electrical energy → light energy / heat energy

For a clockwork toy

strain (potential) energy → kinetic energy

For a family car it might be → sound energy

chemical energy → kinetic energy / heat and sound energy

Other examples of energy transfer

Energy input	Device	Energy output
electrical energy	electric motor	kinetic energy (mechanical work)
chemical energy	candle	heat and light energy
sound energy	microphone	electrical energy
chemical energy	cell or battery	electrical energy
electrical energy	radio	sound energy
potential (strain) energy	clockwork car	kinetic energy
kinetic energy (mechanical work)	generator or dynamo	electrical energy
heat energy	hot air balloon	gravitational potential energy
light energy	tree	chemical energy
chemical energy	match head	heat and light energy
chemical energy	car	kinetic and heat energy

A2 Energy (2)

MAKING ELECTRICITY .... THE POWER STATION

Electrical energy is one of the most convenient forms of energy. At a power station, chemical, nuclear or kinetic energy is converted into electrical energy which is then transmitted through the National Grid to our homes.

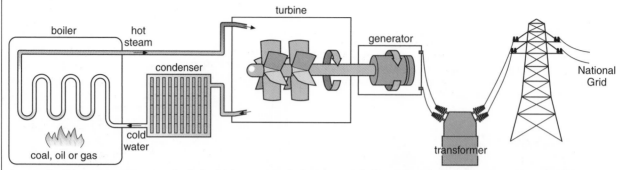

At a coal, oil or gas power station the fuel which contains chemical energy is burned in order to release its energy as heat. This energy is then used to produce steam which turns the turbines to make electricity. In a nuclear power station it is a nuclear reaction that releases the energy to produce the steam.

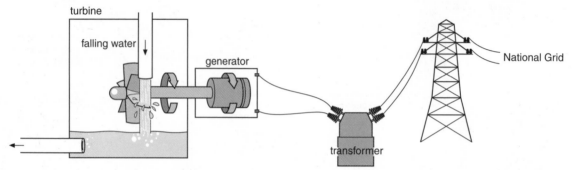

At a hydroelectric power station the flowing water is used to drive the turbines and the generators in order to produce electricity.

EFFICIENCY

Often when energy transformations take place some energy is wasted. The purpose of a bulb is to provide light energy (but it gets hot too).

A bulb which emitted only light would be described as being 100% efficient.

In practice however bulbs also emit heat energy.

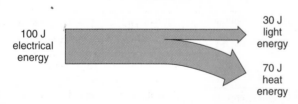

For every 100 J of electrical energy which enter the bulb only 30 J of useful (light) energy are produced.

The efficiency of any energy transfer can be calculated using;

$$\text{efficiency} = \frac{\text{useful energy output}}{\text{energy input}} \times 100\%$$

The efficiency of the bulb is therefore:

$$\text{efficiency} = \frac{30 \text{ J}}{100 \text{ J}} \times 100\% = 30\%$$

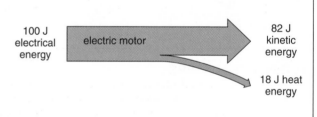

$$\text{efficiency of electric motor} = \frac{82 \text{ J}}{100 \text{ J}} \times 100\% = 82\%$$

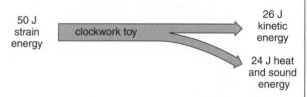

$$\text{efficiency of clockwork toy} = \frac{26 \text{ J}}{50 \text{ J}} \times 100\% = 52\%$$

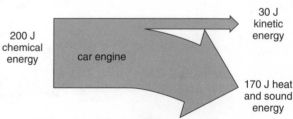

$$\text{efficiency of car engine} = \frac{30 \text{ J}}{200 \text{ J}} \times 100\% = 15\%$$

A3 Energy resources

Most of our energy on Earth comes from the Sun. This energy is generated in a nuclear reaction. Two light elements combine to produce a heavier element accompanied by a release of large quantities of energy.

As this radiant energy (heat and light) reaches the Earth it is converted into other forms.

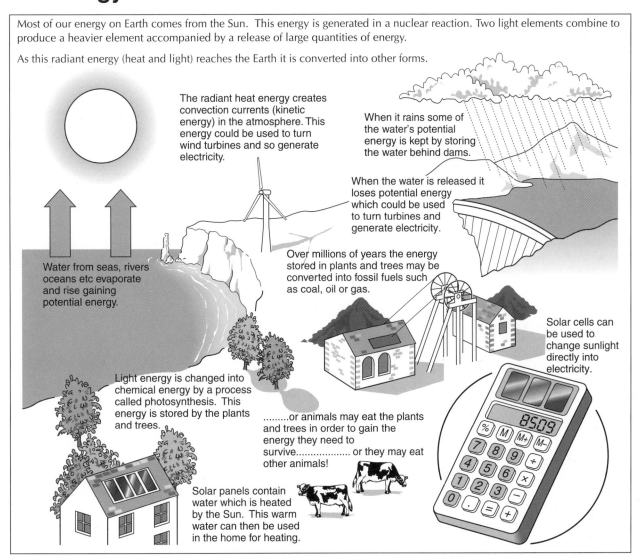

The radiant heat energy creates convection currents (kinetic energy) in the atmosphere. This energy could be used to turn wind turbines and so generate electricity.

When it rains some of the water's potential energy is kept by storing the water behind dams.

When the water is released it loses potential energy which could be used to turn turbines and generate electricity.

Water from seas, rivers oceans etc evaporate and rise gaining potential energy.

Over millions of years the energy stored in plants and trees may be converted into fossil fuels such as coal, oil or gas.

Solar cells can be used to change sunlight directly into electricity.

Light energy is changed into chemical energy by a process called photosynthesis. This energy is stored by the plants and trees.

.........or animals may eat the plants and trees in order to gain the energy they need to survive.................. or they may eat other animals!

Solar panels contain water which is heated by the Sun. This warm water can then be used in the home for heating.

FOSSIL FUELS

Much of the energy an industrial nation such as the UK needs for transport and manufacturing comes from **fossil fuels** such as **coal**, **oil** and **gas**. About 300 million years ago when plants, trees, and animals died they became covered by other plants growing above them and dying. This process happened many, many times. Now deep down in the Earth, these remains were subject to high temperatures and large pressures which over millions of years changed them into fossil fuels. Because it takes so long to make these fuels it is not possible to replace them, they are **non-renewable fuels**.

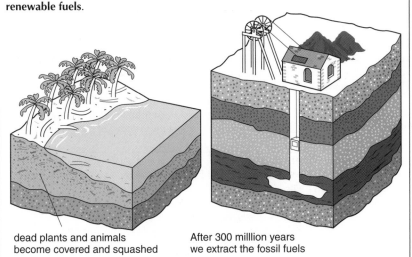

dead plants and animals become covered and squashed

After 300 milllion years we extract the fossil fuels

ENERGY CRISIS

Although energy is never actually lost it frequently ends up in a dilute form which is not very useful. For example, the kinetic energy of a car originates from the fuel it uses. When the car stops much of this energy is transformed into thermal or heat energy in the surroundings.

If we continue to use concentrated forms of energy such as fossil fuels at the present rate there is a real danger that there will be an energy shortfall early next century. There are two possible ways we could avoid or reduce the effect of this shortfall.

- conserve energy by reducing our demands: increase the efficiency of all machines; reduce heat loss from buildings by greater usage of insulation; reuse and recycle objects and materials rather than throwing them away once they have been used.

- make greater use of **alternative sources of energy**.

A4 Alternative sources of energy

SOURCE OF ENERGY	ADVANTAGES AND DISADVANTAGES
Solar energy Radiant energy from the Sun can be captured in several different ways: 1 solar cells convert the radiant energy into electricity eg replace batteries in calculators 2 solar panels ... water passing through the panels is heated by the Sun 3 solar furnaces ... an array of concave mirrors concentrates the Suns ray's creating temperatures in excess of 3000 °C	*Advantages:* • no pollution • renewable source of energy *Disadvantages:* • of limited use in places where there is not continuous sunshine • the initial costs can be very high
Wind energy The kinetic energy of the wind is used to drive wind turbines and generate electricity. Often the turbines are built in clusters ... nicknamed *wind farms*.	*Advantages:* • renewable source of energy • excellent source for isolated communities • low level technology (developing countries) *Disadvantages:* • cause visual and noise pollution • windy site essential • efficiency of energy capture/transfer is very low though more efficient turbines are being developed
Hydroelectric energy Water is collected/stored behind dams usually on high ground such as mountains or hills. It is then released through sluices or pipes and its kinetic energy used to drive generators and produce electricity.	*Advantages:* • renewable source of energy • no pollution *Disadvantages:* • limited number of suitable sites • high initial cost • environmental problems eg flooding of valleys and consequent effect on wildlife
Tidal energy The potential energy of a high tide is stored behind dams and then released at low tide. The flow of water is used to drive generators.	*Advantages:* • renewable source of energy *Disadvantages:* • high initial cost • visual pollution
Wave energy The rocking motion of waves is used to generate electricity.	*Advantages:* • renewable source of energy *Disadvantage:* • very inefficient capture of energy • very large area needed to capture enough energy to be viable....visual pollution
Geothermal energy Nuclear reactions deep in the Earth create high temperatures. Cold water which is pumped through pipes becomes so hot it boils and the steam produced on its return to the surface is used to drive turbines and generate electricity.	*Advantages:* • renewable source of energy *Disadvantages:* • limited number of suitable sites • high cost of drilling deep into the Earth
Biomass Wood is a renewable fuel. When burned it releases its energy. New trees can then be planted to replace those cut down. Sugar cane can be grown and the sugar fermented to produce alcohol which can be used as a fuel instead of petrol.	*Advantages:* • renewable source of energy • low level technology ... good for developing countries *Disadvantages:* • possible pollution and damage to ozone layer • large areas of land will need used to produce enough biomass. This may affect the ecology of the environment
Nuclear energy (fusion) When uranium-235 absorbs a neutron it becomes unstable , splits into two smaller atoms and releases a large amount of energy. This energy is used to turn water into steam to drive turbines and produce electricity.	*Advantages:* • small amounts of fuel produce large amounts of energy *Disadvantages:* • because of the dangers of radioactivity there is the need for very costly, high level safety precautions • the treatment of spent fuel and the decommisioning of nuclear power stations is extremely expensive

A5 Work and power

WORK

In everyday life the word work has many different meanings but to scientists it is something very precise.

Work is done when a force causes an object to move or prevents it from moving. The amount of work done can be calculated using the equation

> work done = force × distance moved in the direction of the force

In order to raise the weights above his head this athlete must apply a force which causes them to move. In doing so he is doing work.

The work done by the athlete above is:

work done = force × distance moved

work done = 2000 N × 2.5 m

work done = 5000 J

In order to cut the lawn this lady must push her lawnmower. As she does so she is doing work.

The work done by the gardner above is:

work done = force × distance moved

work done = 50 N × 40 m

work done = 2000 J

If a force of 1 N causes an object to move 1 m then 1 J (joule) of work has been done

POWER

Power is a measure of how rapidly work is being done. It is measured in watts (W).

$$\text{power} = \frac{\text{work done}}{\text{time taken}}$$

The power of the athlete above is:

$$\text{power} = \frac{\text{work done}}{\text{time taken}}$$

$$\text{power} = \frac{5000 \text{ J}}{0.5 \text{ s}}$$

power = 10000 W or 10 kW

The power of the gardner above is:

$$\text{power} = \frac{\text{work done}}{\text{time taken}}$$

$$\text{power} = \frac{2000 \text{ J}}{200 \text{ s}}$$

power = 100 W

If a person or machine is doing 1 J of work each second their power rating is **1 W** (**watt**).

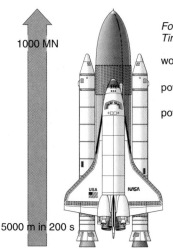

1000 MN

5000 m in 200 s

Force developed from rocket motors = 1 000 000 000 N
Time to travel 5000 m = 200 s

work done = 1 000 000 000 N × 5000 m
= 5 000 000 000 000 J

$$\text{power of motors} = \frac{5\,000\,000\,000\,000 \text{ J}}{200 \text{ s}}$$

power of motors = 25 000 000 000 W

work done = 400 N × 4
= 1600 J
Time to lift load = 8 s

$$\text{power of lifting motor} = \frac{1600 \text{ J}}{8 \text{ s}}$$

power of lifting motor = 2000 W
or   2 kW

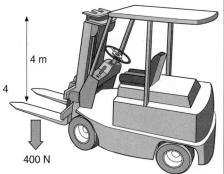

4 m

400 N

A6 Potential energy and kinetic energy

POTENTIAL ENERGY

When the acrobat above jumps down on to the see-saw he propels (lifts) his partner upwards. In doing so he is doing work and therefore must possess energy. The acrobat has energy because of his position. He would be unable to lift his partner if he was also standing on the ground. Energy possessed by an object because of its position (height above the ground) is called **gravitational potential energy**.

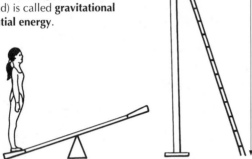

mass 70 kg

3 m

This can be calculated using the formula:

potential energy (PE) $= m \times g \times h$

Where
m = mass of object
g = acceleration due to gravity (9.81 m/s^2)
h = height above the ground

In the case of the acrobat

PE = 70 kg $\times$ 9.81 m/s^2 $\times$ 3 m

PE = 2060 J

The acrobat in order to gain potential energy had to climb to the top of his stand. In doing so he did work. The amount of work he did was equal to the potential energy he gained.

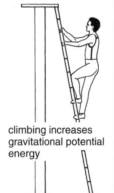

climbing increases gravitational potential energy

STRAINED POTENTIAL ENERGY

Sometimes an object can posses potential energy because of the shape it is in.

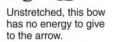

Unstretched, this bow has no energy to give to the arrow.

When the bow is stretched it possesses strained potential energy which it can give to the arrow.

KINETIC ENERGY

When the acrobat opposite is about to land on the see-saw he has lost nearly all his potential energy. It has been converted into kinetic energy. Kinetic energy is the energy a body possesses because of its motion. The kinetic energy of an object can be calculated using the equation.

kinetic energy (KE) $= \frac{1}{2}\, mv^2$

Where
m = mass of object
v = velocity of object

If the acrobat has a mass of 70 kg and as he lands on the see-saw he is falling at a velocity of 7.7 m/s his kinetic energy is

KE $= \frac{1}{2} \times$ 70 kg $\times$ (7.7)^2 m/s^2

$\quad$ = 2060 J

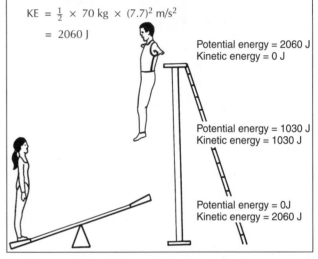

Potential energy = 2060 J
Kinetic energy = 0 J

Potential energy = 1030 J
Kinetic energy = 1030 J

Potential energy = 0J
Kinetic energy = 2060 J

CONSERVATION OF ENERGY

Energy is neither created nor destroyed but can be converted from one form into another.

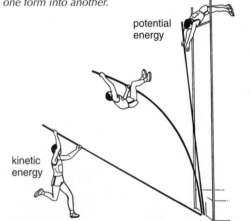

potential energy

kinetic energy

If a pole-vaulter sprints down a runway, just before planting the pole he will possess a lot of kinetic energy. Using the pole, he can convert this energy into potential energy, so lifting himself up and over the bar. In an ideal situation his kinetic energy at the end of his run up ($\frac{1}{2}mv^2$) should be equal to his potential energy (*mgh*) as he clears the bar.

$\frac{1}{2}\, mv^2 = mgh$

Calculate the maximum height a vaulter might clear if his velocity as he plants the pole is 10 m/s

$\frac{1}{2}\, mv^2 = mgh$

$h = \dfrac{\frac{1}{2} \times 10^2}{9.81}$

$h = 5.1$ m

B1 Conduction

CONDUCTION

Conduction is the transfer of energy through an object without its atoms changing position.

The particles at the lower end of this metal rod receive energy from the fire. This energy causes them to vibrate more vigorously.

This extra movement disturbs neighbouring particles causing them to vibrate more vigorously. They become 'warm'.

Over a period of time this extra vibration travels the whole length of the bar. Energy is conducted along it.

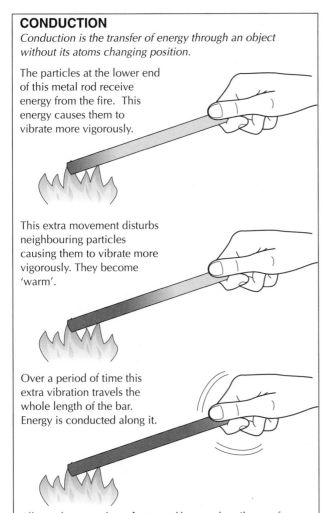

All metal are good **conductors** of heat and easily transfer energy from place to place.
Non metals such as wood, plastics, and ceramics are poor conductors because their particles have very little freedom and are unable to take part in the conduction.

Materials which prevent or restrict heat transfer by conduction are called thermal **insulators**.

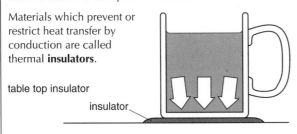

table top insulator

insulator

If a piece of paper is wrapped around a bar which is half wood /half metal and heated gently the paper in contact with the wood turns brown. The paper in contact with the metal remains undamaged. This happens because the metallic half of the bar allows heat from the paper to pass through it and escape. The paper does not get too hot and burn. The heat absorbed by the paper in contact with the wood cannot escape as wood is a poor conductor. The paper becomes too hot and burns .

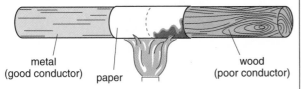

metal
(good conductor)   paper   wood
(poor conductor)

CHOOSING THE RIGHT MATERIAL FOR THE JOB

Heat transfers easily through the metal pan to warm the food. The insulated handle, however, remains cool.

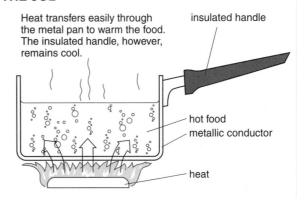

insulated handle

hot food
metallic conductor

heat

Conduction in liquids

Most liquids are poor *conductors* of heat.

Water is such a poor conductor that it is possible to have frozen water and boiling water in the same boiling tube separated by just a few centimetres.

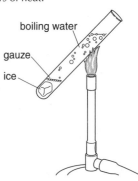

boiling water

gauze

ice

Conduction in gases

Gases are very poor *conductors* of heat. They are in fact excellent insulators and are often used to prevent or reduce the movement of heat by conduction.

Examples of this insulating ability can be seen in the structure of:

*   clothing such as woollen pullovers and string vests

    It is the air trapped within the clothing which reduces the heat loss from our bodies and keeps us warm.

*   glass fibre. This is used to insulate lofts or lag water pipes to stop them from freezing in cold weather. It has large quantities of air trapped between its fibres which reduce heat loss.

*   double glazing

    Glass is a poor conductor of heat but it is the thin layer of air trapped between the two sheets which makes double glazing a very efficient means of reducing heat loss through windows.

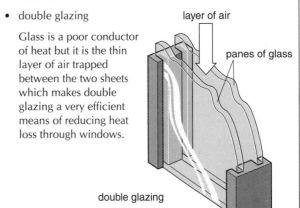

layer of air

panes of glass

double glazing

CONDUCTION THROUGH A VACUUM

It is not possible for heat to travel by conduction through a vacuum as there are no particles present in a vacuum. For this reason a vacuum can be used stop heat flow by conduction (Thermos flask page B3).

B2 Convection

CONVECTION IN FLUIDS (GASES AND LIQUIDS)

Convection is the movement of heat energy by the changing of position of its particles. Convection can only take place in fluids (liquids and gases).

Convection

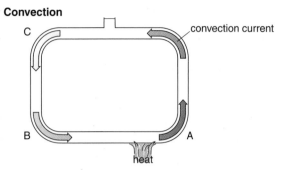

As the liquid at A is heated the particles here gain energy and vibrate more vigorously.

The distance between these particles increases, the liquid becomes less dense.

Cooler, more dense liquid moves in from B forcing the less dense liquid to rise.

Away from the heat source the liquid at C begins to cool, becomes more dense and so returns to the heat source to be warmed once more. This movement of heat energy (and liquid), driven by a heat source, is called a **convection current**.

Domestic hot water systems

Some of the older domestic hot water systems depend upon convection currents to carry hot water from a boiler to the other rooms in the house.

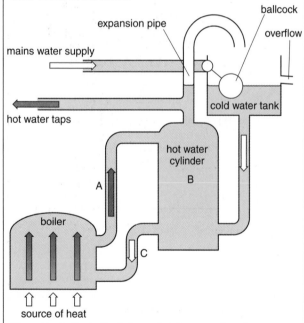

The water in the boiler is heated. It becomes less dense. Cooler, more dense water flows down through pipe C forcing the warmer water to rise through pipe A into the top of the hot water storage tank at B. (This tank is usually found on the first or second floor of most buildings) If the water is unused it will gradually cool, become more dense and fall to the bottom of the storage tank at B before flowing back to the boiler through pipe C to be reheated. If hot water is used the space created is filled by cold water from the mains supply which enters the system through the cold water tank in the loft.

EXAMPLES OF CONVECTION

Convection in gases

Sea breezes along the coast are often convection currents set up by the heat from the sun.

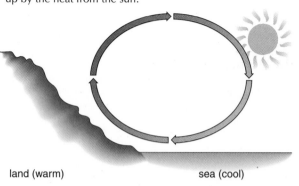

land (warm)   sea (cool)

During the day time the land becomes warmer than the sea. The air immediately above it becomes warm and becomes less dense. Cooler more dense air from over the sea moves in forcing the warmer less dense air to rise. During the daytime there is an onshore breeze.

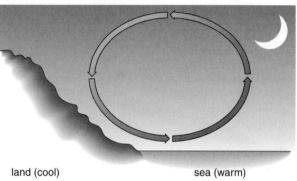

land (cool)   sea (warm)

After the sun has set the land cools down more quickly than the sea and after some hours it is the sea which is the warmer. The air immediately above the sea now rises. The cooler, more dense air over the land forces the warmer, less dense air above the sea to rise. The breeze is now off-shore.

Convection currents in ovens and freezers

In an oven the burners are put at the bottom so that convection currents carry the heat to all parts.

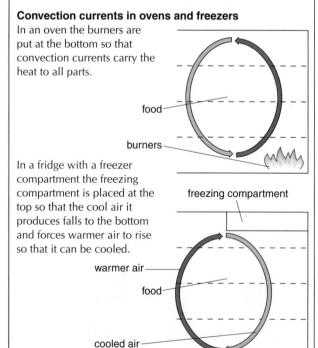

In a fridge with a freezer compartment the freezing compartment is placed at the top so that the cool air it produces falls to the bottom and forces warmer air to rise so that it can be cooled.

B3 Radiation

RADIATION

Radiation is the movement of heat energy by electromagnet waves. It does not involve the movement of particles and is therefore the only means by which heat can travel through a vacuum. All the energy we receive from the sun travels as electromagnetic waves.

ABSORBING RADIATION

When radiation strikes the surface of an object some of it will be absorbed, making the object warmer; some of it will be reflected. The nature of the surface determines the proportions of each.

If the surface is smooth and light coloured most of the radiation will be reflected. If the surface is dark and rough most of the radiation will be absorbed.

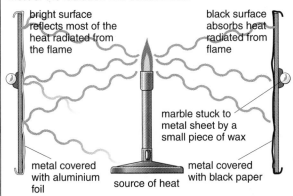

bright surface reflects most of the heat radiated from the flame

black surface absorbs heat radiated from flame

marble stuck to metal sheet by a small piece of wax

metal covered with aluminium foil

source of heat

metal covered with black paper

The marble falls from the back of the dark plate first as it is the better absorber of radiation.

There are many situations in everday life where we make use of this:

- houses in hot countries are painted white to reflect most of the sunlight and remain cool.

- the surfaces and pipes of solar panels are painted black so that they absorb most of the radiation which strikes them and so warm the water.

EMITTERS OF RADIATION

All objects give off heat in the form of radiation. They are emitters. How rapidly they emit heat energy depends upon:
- their temperature ... the hotter they are the greater the rate at which they emit the radiation.
- the nature of their surfaces.
  Objects which are dark and rough are good radiators. Objects which are smooth and light coloured are poor radiators.

Leslie's cube

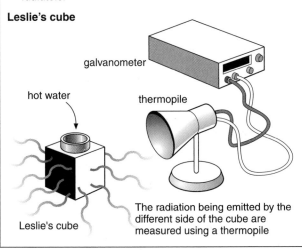

galvanometer

hot water

thermopile

Leslie's cube

The radiation being emitted by the different side of the cube are measured using a thermopile

HEAT TRANSFER ... PRACTICAL APPLICATIONS

The Thermos flask

This is designed to reduce heat flow so that it can be used to keep things hot or cold. If the flask contained for example hot soup:

- heat energy moving by conduction or convection would be stopped by the vacuum.

- any heat crossing the vacuum as radiation would be reflected back by the silvered surfaces.

- the silvered surfaces also reduce the amount of heat being radiated across the vacuum.

- the stopper is made of plastic or cork both of which are excellent insulators.

- the flask itself is protected by an outer casing made of plastic.

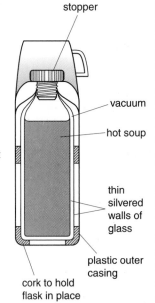

stopper

vacuum

hot soup

thin silvered walls of glass

plastic outer casing

cork to hold flask in place

Insulating the home

The diagram below gives some idea of how heat energy might escape from a house if there was no insulation.

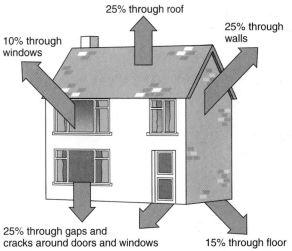

25% through roof

10% through windows

25% through walls

25% through gaps and cracks around doors and windows

15% through floor

The following methods could be used to reduce this loss of heat:

- insulate the loft with glass fibre

- double glaze all windows

- inject foam between the cavity walls to reduce convection currents carrying heat across the gap

- fit underlay and carpets in all ground floor rooms

- fit draft excluders and/or curtains to doors and windows

Radiators in the home!

Many modern houses are heated by radiators. Hot water is passed through which then warms the rooms...... by creating *convection currents*. Although some heat is radiated into the room it is only a small amount. Most domestic radiators are painted white and light coloured surfaces are poor emitters of heat radiation.

B4 Thermal expansion and contraction

When large structures such as buildings and bridges are designed, great care must be taken to allow for the expansion and contraction that will take place as their temperatures change.

As the temperature of a structure increases its particles gain energy and vibrate more vigorously. This increased movement results in expansion. If the temperature decreases the particles lose energy, vibrate less, and the structure contracts.

The amount an object expands or contracts depends upon:
- the size of the object ... the expansion of a solid is relatively small. The effects are often only noticeable if the object is large.
- the temperature change.
- the material from which the object is made. A one metre bar of steel which is warmed by 1 °C will expand by 0.00001 m but a one bar of aluminium warmed by the same amount will expand three times as much.

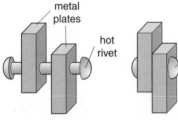

combs like these allow the road to expand and contract unnoticed by the drivers

roller

The Firth of Forth bridge is approximately 1m longer in the summer than in the winter. If no account was taken of this, the forces of expansion are large enough to cause the bridge to buckle.

THERMOSTAT

A thermostat is a switch which is used to control temperature: the temperature in a room; in an oven; or the temperature of a steam iron.

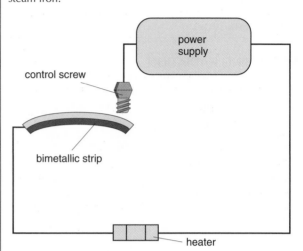

power supply

control screw

bimetallic strip

heater

When the heater is turned on the bimetallic strip is straight, the contacts are touching and the circuit is complete. As the strip becomes warmer it bends downwards until the contacts are broken. The heater is now turned off, the temperature begins to fall and the strip begins to straighten. When the contacts meet the circuit is complete and the heater is turned on. This constant turning on and off of the heater by the strip keeps the temperature fairly constant. If a higher temperature is required the temperature control screw is turned to push the contacts together more firmly so a higher temperature is required before the strip bends enough to break the heating circuit.

USES OF THERMAL EXPANSION AND CONTRACTION
Riveting

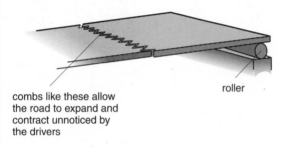

metal plates

hot rivet

when the hot rivets cool down they contract pulling the plates together so firmly that they form a watertight seal

Bimetallic strip
A bimetallic strip consists of two metals stuck or riveted together. The two metals are chosen such that one expands a great deal more than the other when heated. As a result the bimetallic strip bends with the metal that expands the most on the outside of the curve. If the strip is allowed to cool and contract it will once again become straight.

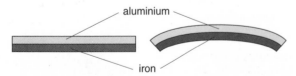

aluminium

iron

(a) bimetallic strip when cool　　(b) bimetallic strip when warm

This changing of shape with temperature makes the bimetallic strip very useful in temperature sensing devices such as fire alarms and thermostats.

THERMOMETERS
Most liquids and gases expand and contract far more than solids for the same change in temperature. This property is made use of in thermometers.

Thermometers measure how hot or how cold an object is

Mercury-in-glass thermometer
As the mercury in the bulb is heated it becomes warm and expands up the narrow capillary tube. The higher the temperature the further the mercury column rises.

Mercury is used in thermometers because:
- it expands regularly with change in temperature
- it can be used over a wide range of temperatures ie 350 °C – –40 °C.
- it is clearly visible even in the narrow capillary tube.

constriction prevents the mercury from returning to the bulb once it has been removed from the patient's mouth

restricted scale for more accurate readings

43 °C

a clinical thermometer

35 °C

bulb

Mercury is quite expensive and poisonous. Alcohol is therefore sometimes used as an alternative. It is cheaper and can be used to read much lower temperatures than the mercury thermometer but it can not be used to measure higher temperatures. Alcohol is a colourless liquid so a dye is added to it to make it visible.

B5 Gas laws (1)

If a solid or a liquid is heated it will in most cases expand as its temperature increases. With gases this may or may not happen. It is possible that the volume of the gas may remain constant and it is the pressure of the gas which changes. The relationships between the pressure, volume and temperature of a gas are described by three gas laws.

CHARLES'S LAW

To investigate the relationship between the volume and temperature of a gas whilst its pressure is kept constant.

A fixed mass of air, at atmospheric pressure, is trapped inside a capillary tube by a small bead of sulphuric acid. The tube is heated using a water bath. The temperature and volume of the air are noted at regular intervals.

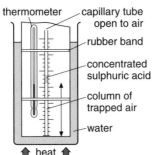

Typical Results

Volume/ cm^3	Temperature/ °C	Temperature/ K	V/T
20.0	15	288	0.0694
21.4	35	308	0.0694
23.5	65	338	0.0694
23.8	80	343	0.0694
26.1	90	376	0.0694

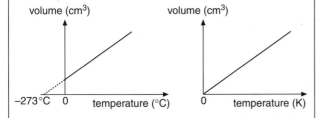

Charles's law
The volume of a fixed mass of gas is directly proportional to its temperature providing the pressure remains constant.

Charles's Law can also be expressed in the form of an equation

$$\frac{V_1}{T_1} = \frac{V_2}{T_2}$$ *(T$_1$ and T$_2$ must be in degrees Kelvin)*

Example
A mass of gas has a volume of 400 cm^3 at 27 °C. What will be the volume of this gas at 327 °C providing that the pressure remains constant?

Using: $\frac{V_1}{T_1} = \frac{V_2}{T_2}$

$$\frac{400}{(27 + 273)} = \frac{V_2}{(327 + 273)}$$

$$V_2 = \frac{400 \times 600}{300}$$

$$V_2 = 800 \text{ cm}^3$$

PRESSURE LAW

To investigate the relationship between the pressure of a gas and its temperature whilst the volume is kept constant.

A fixed mass of gas is heated using a water bath. The temperature and the pressure of the gas are noted at regular intervals.

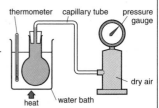

Typical Results

Pressure/ Pa	Temperature/ °C	Temperature/ K	P/T
110 000	15	288	381.9
115 715	30	303	381.9
121 444	45	318	381.9
123 354	50	323	381.9
127 173	60	333	381.9

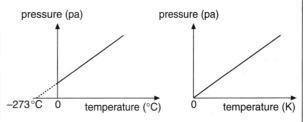

The table and the straight line graphs above confirm the

Pressure law
The pressure of a fixed mass of gas is directly proportional to its temperature providing the volume remains constant.

The Pressure law can also be expressed in the form of an equation

$$\frac{P_1}{T_1} = \frac{P_2}{T_2}$$

(T$_1$ and T$_2$ must be in degrees Kelvin)

Pressure law continued on page 16.

Charles's law and the kinetic theory
If the temperature (in Kelvin) of a gas doubles, the number of times the particles hit the sides of the container per second also doubles. If the pressure of the gas is to remain constant its volume must double.

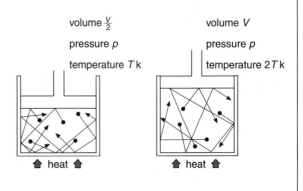

B6 Gas laws (2)

PRESSURE LAW CONTINUED

Example

A tin can contains air at a pressure of 100000 Pa and a temperature of 7 °C. Calculate the pressure of the air if the can is heated to a temperature of 77 °C.

Using:

$$\frac{P_1}{T_1} = \frac{P_2}{T_2}$$

$$\frac{100\,000}{(7 + 273)} = \frac{P_2}{(77 + 273)}$$

$$P_2 = \frac{100\,000 \times 350}{280}$$

$$P_2 = 125\,000 \text{ Pa}$$

Pressure law and the kinetic theory

If the temperature of a gas doubles, the number of times the particles hit the sides of the container each second also doubles. The pressure of the gas doubles providing there is no change in volume.

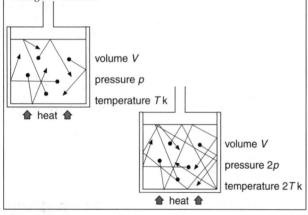

BOYLE'S LAW

To investigate the relationship between the volume of a gas and its pressure whilst its temperature is kept constant.

A fixed mass of gas is trapped in a glass tube. Using a footpump pressure is applied to the gas through a column of oil. The pressure of the gas can be see on the pressure gauge whilst the volume of the gas is shown at the side of the tube. The experiment is repeated over a range of pressures and the results noted in a table.

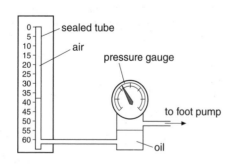

Typical Results

Pressure/Pa	Volume/cm^2	$P \times V$
110 000	50	5 500 000
137 500	40	5 500 000
183 333	30	5 500 000
275 000	20	5 500 000
550 000	10	5 500 000

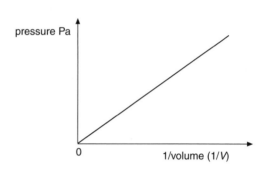

The table and the straight line graphs you obtain when pressure is plotted against 1/volume confirm that there is an *inverse relationship* between the pressure of a gas and its volume.

Boyle's law

The volume of a fixed mass of gas is inversely proportional to its pressure providing the temperature is kept constant.

Boyle's law can also be expressed in the form of an equation

$$P_1 \times V_1 = P_2 \times V_2$$

Example

What will be the final pressure of a 500 cm^3 of air at 100000 Pa if it is squashed to one fifth of its original volume without changing its temperature?

Using:

$$P_1 \times V_1 = P_2 \times V_2$$

$$100000 \times 500 = P_2 \times 100$$

$$P_2 = \frac{100\,000 \times 500}{100}$$

$$P_2 = 500\,000 \text{ Pa}$$

Boyle's law and the kinetic theory

If the volume which a sample of gas occupies is doubled the number of times the particles hit the sides of the container per second halves. The pressure of the gas halves providing there is no change in temperature.

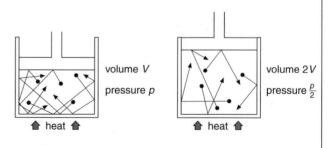

C1 Speed and velocity

SPEED

This arrow travels 50 m each second it is in flight.
Its speed is 50 m/s

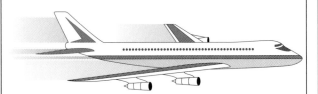

This aeroplane travels 1000 km each hour it is in flight.
Its speed is 1000 km/h

The speed of any object can be found using the equation:

$$\text{speed} = \frac{\text{distance travelled}}{\text{time taken}}$$

Example
An athlete runs 400 m in 60 s. Calculate the speed.

$$\text{speed} = \frac{\text{distance travelled}}{\text{time taken}}$$

$$\text{speed} = \frac{400 \text{ m}}{60 \text{ s}}$$

$$\text{speed} = 6.66 \text{ m/s}$$

Example
A cheetah runs at a speed of 20 m/s for 50 s. Calculate how far it will have travelled in this time.

$$\text{speed} = \frac{\text{distance travelled}}{\text{time taken}}$$

So:

distance travelled = speed × time taken

distance travelled = 20 m/s × 50 s

distance travelled = 1000 m

In these examples it is assumed that all the speeds are constant but in everyday life this is rarely the case. The walker may slow down slightly when walking uphill and speed up when walking downhill. The equation above might be more accurately written as.

$$\text{average speed} = \frac{\text{total distance travelled}}{\text{time taken}}$$

A bus takes 40 mins to complete its 24 km route. Calculate its average speed.

$$\text{average speed} = \frac{\text{total distance travelled}}{\text{time taken}}$$

$$\text{average speed} = \frac{24000 \text{ m}}{40 \times 60 \text{ s}}$$

$$\text{average speed} = 10 \text{ m/s}$$

SPEED AND VELOCITY

In everyday life the words **speed** and **velocity** are often used as if they mean the same. To a scientist there is a difference. The story below illustrates this difference.

Two trains were travelling along the same single railway track. One was travelling at 100 km/h and the other at 101 km/h. The two trains collided. Very few of the passengers realised that there had been a crash, no one was injured and both trains continued on to their final destinations.

On the following day another two trains were travelling along the same stretch of tracks at the same speeds. This time when the trains collided everyone knew what had happened. Many people were injured and both trains left the track. How can two apparently identical situations give rise to two totally different results?

To solve this problem it is necessary to realise that a vital piece of information has been withheld. To be able to predict the outcome of the collision, it is necessary to know not only the speed of each of the trains but also their directions. In the first collision both trains were travelling in the same direction. The collision speed was therefore 1 km/h (101 km/h –100 km/h). In the second collision the trains were travelling in opposite directions. The collision speed was therefore 201 km/h 101 km/h + 100 km/h).

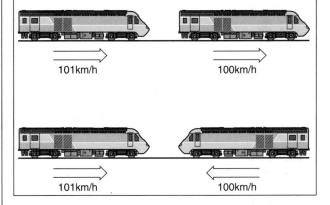

101km/h   100km/h

101km/h   100km/h

SCALARS AND VECTORS

The speed of an object only indicates how fast it is moving. The velocity of an object provides two pieces of information ie the object's speed and its direction. In the example above the speeds of the trains are 101 km/h and 100 km/h whilst their velocities are 101 km/h towards and 100 km/h away.

Measurements or quantities which provide information about size (magnitude) such as distance, speed, mass etc are called **scalars**. Measurements or quantities which provide two pieces of information (magnitude *and* direction) such as velocity, acceleration, force etc are called **vectors**.

Examples of vectors

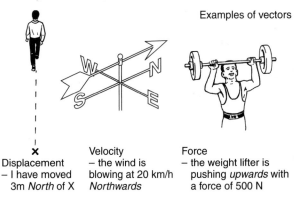

×
Displacement
– I have moved
3m *North* of X

Velocity
– the wind is
blowing at 20 km/h
Northwards

Force
– the weight lifter is
pushing *upwards* with
a force of 500 N

C2 Acceleration

If an object increases its velocity it is **accelerating**. If an object decreases its velocity it is **decelerating**. The size of an acceleration can be calculated using the equation:

$$acceleration = \frac{change\ in\ velocity}{time\ taken}$$

or

$$a = \frac{v - u}{t}$$

where a is acceleration

u is initial speed

v is final speed

t is time taken

Example
A cyclist accelerates from rest to 10m/s in 5s. Calculate her acceleration.

Using:

$$a = \frac{v - u}{t}$$

$$a = \frac{10\ m/s - 0\ m/s}{5\ s}$$

$$a = 2\ m/s^2$$

On average this cylist increases her speed by 2 m/s each second.

Example
A sprinter after crossing the finishing line at a speed of 8 m/s needs 4 s to come to rest. Calculate his deceleration.

Using:

$$a = \frac{v - u}{t}$$

$$a = \frac{0\ m/s - 8\ m/s}{4\ s}$$

$$a = -2\ m/s^2$$

The sprinter has a deceleration of 2 m/s².

ACCELERATION DUE TO GRAVITY

One of the most common ways in which an object can accelerate is by falling. Objects fall because of the gravitational attraction between the object and the Earth. In the absence of friction and air resistance all objects fall to Earth with an acceleration of 9.81 m/s². ie $g = 9.81$ m/s². Objects which fall on the Moon have an acceleration of $\frac{1}{6} \times 9.81$ m/s². Objects which fall on the planet Jupiter will have an acceleration of 2.54×9.81 m/s².

Example
Calculate the speed of an object 3 s after it has been dropped
a) on Earth   b) on the Moon   c) on Jupiter

a) Using:

$$a = \frac{v - u}{t}$$

$$9.81\ m/s = \frac{v - 0\ m/s}{3\ s}$$

$$v - 0\ m/s = 9.81\ m/s^2 \times 3\ s$$

$$v = 29.43\ m/s$$

b)

$$v_{Moon} = \frac{9.81\ m/s^2 \times 3\ s}{6}$$

$$v_{Moon} = 4.91\ m/s^2$$

c)

$$v_{Jupiter} = 2.54 \times 9.81\ m/s^2 \times 3\ s$$

$$v_{Jupiter} = 74.75\ m/s^2$$

Experiment to determine the acceleration due to gravity

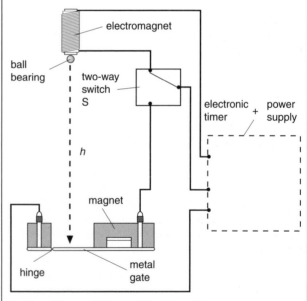

When the two-way switch S is opened the electromagnet is turned off, the ball bearing begins to fall and the electronic timer starts. When the ball bearing strikes the metal gate the timer stops. The distance the ball bearing has fallen and the time displayed by the timer is noted. A value for g is calculated using the equation:

$$g = \frac{2h}{t^2}$$

The whole experiment is repeated with different values of h and an average value of g is calculated from these results.

C3 Equations of motion

Providing an object is moving with uniform velocity or uniform acceleration it is possible to describe its motion using the three equations shown below.

$$v = u + at$$
$$s = ut + \tfrac{1}{2}at^2 \qquad \text{where } s \text{ is the distance travelled}$$
$$v^2 = u^2 + 2as$$

Example
A car travelling at 10 m/s accelerates at the rate of 2 m/s^2 for 15 s. Calculate the final speed of the car and the distance it has travelled during this time.

Using:
$$v = u + at$$
$$v = 10 \text{ m/s} + 2 \text{ m/s}^2 \times 15 \text{ s}$$
$$v = 40 \text{ m/s}$$

Using:
$$v^2 = u^2 + 2as$$
$$s = \frac{v^2 - u^2}{2a}$$
$$s = \frac{40^2 - 10^2}{2 \times 2}$$
$$s = \frac{1600 - 100}{4}$$
$$s = 375 \text{ m}$$

Example
A cylist travelling at 5 m/s accelerates at 1 m/s^2 for 20 s. Calculate how far she has travelled during this time.

Using:
$$s = ut + \tfrac{1}{2}at^2$$
$$s = 5 \times 20 + \tfrac{1}{2} \times 1 \times 20^2$$
$$s = 100 + 200$$
$$s = 300 \text{ m}$$

Example
A ball is thrown vertically upwards with a velocity of 20m/s. Calculate the maximum height that the ball reaches and the total time it is in the air.

Using:
$$v^2 = u^2 + 2as$$
$$0^2 = 20^2 + 2 \times -9.81 \times s$$
$$2 \times 9.81 \times s = 20^2$$
$$s = \frac{400}{2 \times 9.81}$$
$$s = 20.4\text{m}$$

For the upward flight of the ball:

Using:
$$v = u + at$$
$$0 = 20 + -9.81 \times t$$
$$t = \frac{20}{9.81}$$
$$t = 2.04 \text{ s}$$

The downward flight of the ball will take exactly the same time as the upward flight. Therefore the ball will be in the air for a total of (2.04 s + 2.04 s) = 4.08 s.

Example
A ball bearing falls 1 m in 0.45 s. Calculate the acceleration it experiences due to gravity.

The ball starts from rest so:
$$v = u + at$$
$$v = gt$$

If the acceleration of the ball is uniform its average velocity during this time is

$$v_{av} = \frac{gt}{2}$$

But:
$$v_{av} = \frac{\text{distance travelled}}{\text{time taken}}$$
$$= \frac{h}{t}$$

So:
$$\frac{h}{t} = \frac{gt}{2}$$
$$h = \tfrac{1}{2}gt^2$$
$$g = \frac{2h}{t^2}$$
$$g = \frac{2 \times 1}{0.45^2}$$
$$g = 9.81 \text{ m/s}^2$$

C4 Graphs of motion

DISTANCE/TIME GRAPHS

a)

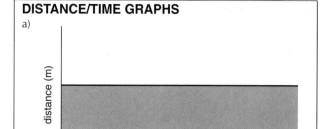

This object is stationary. The distance travelled is not changing with time.

b)

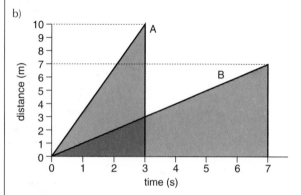

The distances travelled by these objects are changing uniformly with time. ie they are both moving at constant speeds. Their speeds can be calculated from the **gradients** of the graphs.

For object A:

$$\text{gradient} = \frac{10}{3}$$

$$\text{speed} = 3.3 \text{ m/s}$$

For object B:

$$\text{gradient} = \frac{7 \text{ m}}{7 \text{ s}}$$

$$\text{speed} = 1 \text{ m/s}$$

SPEED (VELOCITY) /TIME GRAPHS

a)

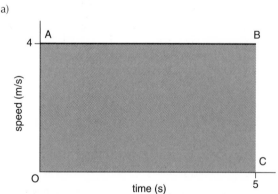

This object is travelling at a constant speed of 4 m/s. The distance it has travelled after a certain time (5s) is equal to the area under the graph (OABC).

$$4 \text{ m/s} \times 5 \text{ s} = 20 \text{ m}$$

b)

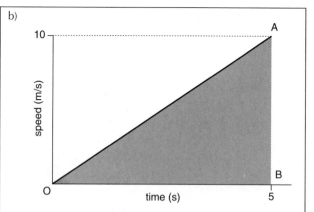

This object has started from rest and increased its speed uniformly. It has a constant acceleration. The distance travelled by the object after time t is given by the area under the graph: triangle OAB.

The **acceleration** of the object is given by the gradient of the graph.

$$\text{gradient} = \frac{AB}{OB}$$

$$\text{gradient} = \frac{10}{5}$$

$$= 2 \text{ m/s}^2$$

c)

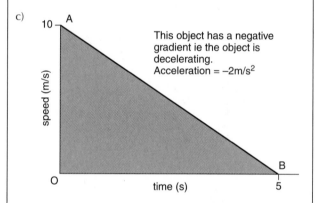

This object has a negative gradient ie the object is decelerating.
Acceleration = -2m/s^2

d)

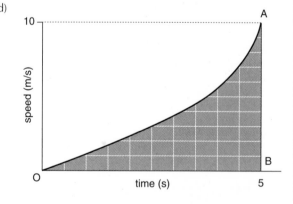

The gradient of this graph is continually changing. The object is not accelerating uniformly. It is accelerating at an increasing rate.

The distance travelled is again equal to the area under the graph ABO. An approximate value can be found by the method of 'counting squares'.

C5 Forces

THE EFFECT OF FORCES

There are many different kinds of force ... pushing, pulling, bending, twisting ...

On most occasions it is necessary to be in contact with an object in order to apply a force to it.

However, forces such as gravitational, electrostatic, and magnetic forces can be applied from a distance.

In general if a force is applied to an object it may:

change the speed of an object

change the direction in which the object is moving

change the shape of an object

How great these effects are depends upon the size of the applied force. The size of a force is measured in **Newtons** (N).

HOOKE'S LAW

A scientist named Robert Hooke carried out many experiments to discover how springs and wires deformed when tensile (stretching) forces were applied to them. The diagrams below represent a summary of his findings.

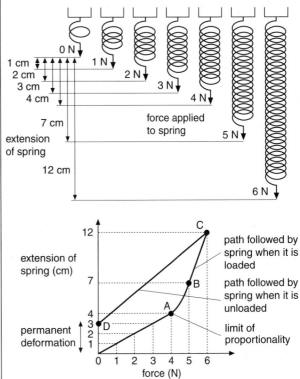

Hooke discovered that providing the extension was not too great the stretching of the spring was proportional to the applied force. If the applied force was doubled the amount by which the spring or wire stretched also doubled.

Hooke's law:

The extension of a piece of wire is directly proportional to the applied force providing the limit of proportionality is not exceeded.

- between O and A Hooke's Law is obeyed.

- beyond A the extension of the wire is no longer proportional to the applied force.

- up to B the wire has deformed elastically ie if the applied forces are removed the spring returns to its original shape.

- beyond B the spring undergoes plastic deformation and will not return to its original size and shape when the applied forces are removed. The spring has been *permanently deformed*.

Newton-meters Because springs stretch uniformly when forces are applied to them they are often used to measure the size of a force.

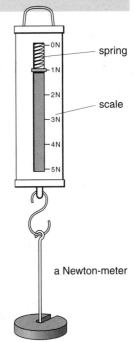

a Newton-meter

C6 Mass, weight, and density

This wrestler on the right is massive compared with his opponent on the left. There is more of him. The mass of an object is a measure of how much there is of it. (In scientific terms it is a measure of how much matter there is.)

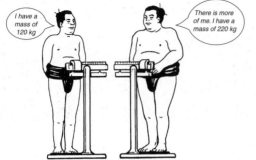

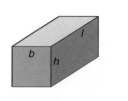

The unit of mass is the kilogram (kg). Mass can be found using a balance.

This wrestler is concerned about his opponent. He is concerned about the *force his mass is applying to him*. In simple terms he is concerned about his weight. The weight of an object is the gravitational attraction it experiences and is measured in **newtons (N)**. The mass of an object and its weight are related by the equation

> weight = mass × acceleration due to gravity
>
> $w = mg$
>
> (where $g = 9.81$ m/s^2 on Earth)

If this contest was to take place on the Moon the masses of the two wrestlers would be unchanged but because the gravitational attraction there is just $\frac{1}{6}$th that on the Earth the smaller wrestler would be slightly less concerned with the weight of his opponent. Similarly on the the planet Jupiter the gravitational attraction is approximately $2\frac{1}{2}$ times that on the Earth so whilst the masses remain the same the wrestlers' weights would be $2\frac{1}{2}$ times that on the Earth.

DENSITY

The density of an object depends upon how tightly its atoms are packed together. The atoms of a metal such as lead are closely packed whilst those of gases are well spaced out. Materials like lead are said to have a high density and gases a low density.

The density of a material can be found using the equation:

$$\text{density} = \frac{\text{mass}}{\text{volume}}$$

Material	Density	Material	Density
lead	11000 kg/m^3	water	1000 kg/m^3
mercury	13600 kg/m^3	Ice	920 kg/m^3
aluminium	2700 kg/m^3	air	1.29 kg/m^3
cork	240 kg/m^3		

To find the density of a regular shaped object

volume = $l \times b \times h$ volume = $\frac{4}{3}\pi r^3$

The object is 'weighed' to find its mass. The dimensions are then measured to find its volume. The density is then calculated using the formula.

To find the density of an iregular shaped object

A eureka can is filled with water and the object lowered into it until it is fully immersed. The displaced water is collected and its volume measured. The volume of the displaced water is the same as the volume of the object. The object is dried and 'weighed' to find its mass. The density is calculated using the formula.

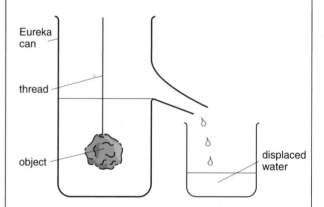

To find the density of a liquid

The volume of the liquid is measured in a measuring cylinder. The mass of the measuring cylinder with and without the liquid are noted and the density calculated using the formula.

To find the density of a gas eg air

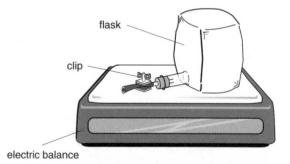

The plastic cube containing the air (gas) is 'weighed' (*mass 1*) and its dimensions measured using a metre rule. The gas is then removed using a vacuum pump or by folding and squashing the cube. The empty cube is now 'weighed' (*mass 2*). The density of the gas is calculated using the modified formula.

$$\text{density} = \frac{mass\ 1 - mass\ 2}{\text{volume}}$$

C7 Forces and motion

NEWTON'S FIRST LAW OF MOTION

Every body continues in its state of uniform motion or rest unless acted up on by an external force.

This shot is stationary.

In order to make it move a force must be applied to it.

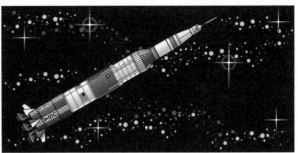

This rocket is *freewheeling* through space ... its motors are not working. But because there are no external forces such as friction acting on it, it will continue indefinitely at the same speed and in the same direction.

INERTIA...CHANGING A BODY'S VELOCITY TAKES TIME

The changes that take place when forces are applied to objects are not always immediate.

It is impossible for these indoor sprinters to apply sufficient forces to themselves to stop immediately they have finished. It takes several seconds for them to slow down and stop.

This bobsleigh team has a similar problem. Only after pushing hard for several seconds do they reach race speed.

it's much more difficult to stop this

it's easy to stop this

Decelerating an object with a large mass is much more difficult than decelerating one with a small mass.

From these two examples you can see that objects cannot be accelerated or decelerated instantaneously. They seem reluctant to change their velocity. We describe this property as **inertia**. The amount of inertia an object possesses depends upon its mass. The greater the mass, the greater the inertia.

If this piece of paper is given a sharp sideways tap it is pushed to one side but the larger inertia of the coin prevents it from moving. If the experiment is repeated with a cardboard disc replacing the coin, both the sheet of card and the disc will move sideways as the disc has a much smaller mass than the coin and therefore a much smaller inertia.

If a car is brought to an abrupt stop eg in an accident its passengers possess inertia which tries to resist this sudden deceleration. The passengers in the car feel as if they are being thrown forward but in fact it is their bodies' reluctance to slow down which causes this lurch forward. The forces required to prevent this are far greater than a human can apply. Hence the importance of seat-belts which can apply sufficiently large restraining forces.

C8 Momentum

All objects that are moving have **momentum**. Objects which are stationary have no momentum. The momentum of an object can be calculated using the equation

momentum = mass (kg) × velocity (m/s)

The units of momentum are kg m/s.

Calculate the momentum of a car of mass 500 kg moving with a velocity of 20 m/s.

Using:

momentum = $m \times v$

momentum = 500 kg × 20 m/s

momentum = 10000 kg m/s

mass of ball = 10 kg

velocity of ball when released = 15 m/s

momentum of ball = 10 kg × 15 m/s

= 150 kg m/s

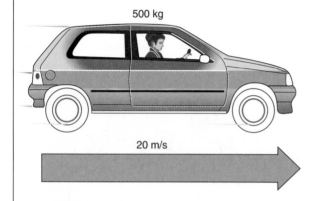

500 kg

20 m/s

mass of bear = 100 kg

velocity of bear = 5 m/s

momentum of bear = 100 kg × 5 m/s

= 500 kg m/s

ADVANCED TOPICS 1

Newton's second law of motion is often stated using momentum.

(see page 25)

$F = m \times a$

But:

$a = \dfrac{v - u}{t}$

So:

$F = \dfrac{m(v - u)}{t}$

$F = \dfrac{(mv - mu)}{t}$

$F = \dfrac{\text{change in momentum}}{\text{time taken}}$

When a force is applied to a body the rate of change of momentum of the body is proportional to the size of the applied force.

Example

A car of mass 600 kg accelerates from rest of 30 m/s in 10 s. Calculate the propulsive force developed by the cars engine.

Using:

$F = \dfrac{mv - mu}{t}$

$F = \dfrac{600 \text{ kg} \times 30 \text{ m/s} - 600 \text{ kg} \times 0}{10 \text{ s}}$

$F = \dfrac{18000 \text{ kg m/s}}{10 \text{ s}}$

$F = 1800 \text{ N}$

ADVANCED TOPICS 2

Conservation of momentum

This states that *if two or more bodies collide the momentum of the bodies before the collision is equal to the momentum of the bodies after collision.*

$m_1v_1 + m_2v_2 = m_1v_3 + m_2v_4$

Example

A locomotive of mass 100 000 kg and travelling with a velocity of 10 m/s collides with a wagon of mass 10000 kg moving with a velocity of 5 m/s in the same direction. After the collision the wagon moves at 15 m/s. What is the velocity of the locomotive?

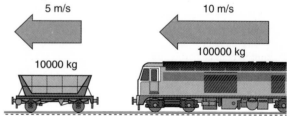

5 m/s

10 m/s

10000 kg

100000 kg

Using:

$m_1v_1 + m_2v_2 = m_1v_3 + m_2v_4$

100 000 kg × 10 m/s + 10 000 kg × 5 m/s

= 100 000 kg × v_3 + 10 000 kg × 15 m/s

1 050 000 kgm/s = 100 000 kg × v_3 + 150 000 kgm/s

900 000 kg m/s = 100 000 kg × v_3

$v_3 = \dfrac{900\,000 \text{ kg m/s}}{100\,000 \text{ kg}}$

$v_3 = 9 \text{ m/s}$

C9 Newton's second and third laws of motion

NEWTON'S SECOND LAW OF MOTION

This describes the relationship between the size of the force applied to an object and the acceleration it produces.

> The acceleration of a body is directly proportional to the applied force and inversely proportional to its mass.

Experiment to confirm the relationship between force, mass, and acceleration.

When the air track is turned on a force F is applied to the trolley. The acceleration of the trolley is measured and the experiment repeated 5 or 6 times more with different values of F.

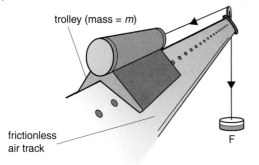

trolley (mass = m)

frictionless
air track

F

The whole experiment is then repeated and the applied force F is kept constant but the mass of the trolley is varied. These experiments confirm that

$$a \propto F \quad \text{and} \quad a \propto \frac{1}{m}$$

These two relationships can be combined in the one equation

$$F = m \times a$$

Example
A bobsleigh of mass 500 kg is pushed at the start with a force of 2000 N. What is its initial acceleration?

$$F = m \times a$$
$$2000 \text{ N} = 500 \text{ kg} \times a$$
$$a = \frac{2000 \text{ N}}{500 \text{ kg}}$$
$$a = 4 \text{ m/s}^2$$

NEWTON'S THIRD LAW OF MOTION

In order to step off her boat this rower must move her body forward. She does this by pushing with her leg muscles. Unfortunately, as she pushes herself forwards she also pushes the boat backwards.

If this disembarking was repeated with different rowers and boats, taking measurements of their masses (m) and their velocities (v) a pattern would emerge. The **momentum** the rower gives herself as she steps off the boat is equal to the **momentum** given to the boat.

$$m_1 \times v_1 = m_2 \times v_2$$

Newton describes this relationship in his Third Law of Motion

To every action there is an equal and opposite reaction.

mass = 160 kg
velocity = 1 m/s

mass = 80 kg
velocity = 2 m/s

Action ... player number 3 pushes player number 21 (mass 160 kg) to the left with a velocity of 1 m/s
Reaction ... player number 3 (mass 80 kg) moves to the right with a velocity of 2 m/s

Rockets and jet engines use this principle to propel themselves.

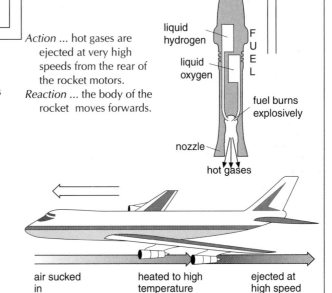

Action ... hot gases are ejected at very high speeds from the rear of the rocket motors.
Reaction ... the body of the rocket moves forwards.

liquid hydrogen

liquid oxygen

FUEL

fuel burns explosively

nozzle

hot gases

air sucked in

heated to high temperature

ejected at high speed

Action ... air is blown out of the jet engines at high speeds
Reaction ... the aircraft moves forwards

In clay pigeon shooting, when the trigger is pulled the shot is ejected at great speed from the barrel whilst the gun itself is made to move in the opposite direction. This reaction to the ejecting of the shot is called *recoil*.

Example
Calculate the recoil velocity of a gun of mass 3 kg if the mass of the shot is 0.3 kg and its velocity as it leaves the barrel is 380 m/s.

$$m_1 \times v_1 = m_2 \times v_2$$
$$0.3 \text{ kg} \times 380 \text{ m/s} = 3\text{kg} \times v_2$$
$$v_2 = 38 \text{ m/s}$$

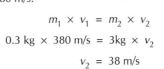

C10 Balanced and unbalanced forces

MORE THAN ONE FORCE

It is rare, in everyday life, that an object experiences the effects of just one force acting upon it.

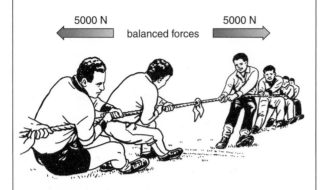

5000 N ← balanced forces → 5000 N

This rope is feeling the effects of two tug of war teams pulling in opposite directions. If the two teams are exerting the same force on the rope, the forces are balanced, there is no resultant force and the rope remains stationary. If however one of the teams applies a larger force than their opponents there is a resultant force and the rope will move in the direction of this force.

Balanced forces (Newton's second law of motion) cause an object:

- to remain stationary

- to continue to move in the same direction and at the same speed

- to possibly change shape.

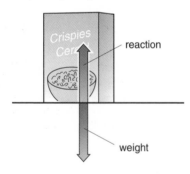

reaction

weight

This box is experiencing the gravitational force we call weight. It is not moving because the table on which it is resting is pushing upwards with an equal and opposite force called **reaction**.

friction

accelerating force downward slope due to weight

This sledge is sliding down a slope at a constant speed because the force due to its weight is balanced by an equal and opposite force called **friction**.

FREE-FALL

As a free-fall parachutist jumps from an aircraft he immediately begins to accelerate at 9.81 m/s² because of the gravitational attraction of the Earth. However, as his speed increases so does his air resistance and his resultant accelerating force gradually decreases. Eventually the frictional forces and the gravitational pull become equal and there is no resultant force and the parachutist falls at a *constant velocity*. This is known as his **terminal velocity**.

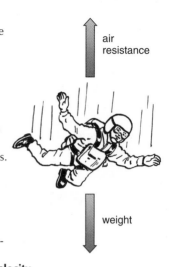

air resistance

weight

velocity (m/s)

terminal velocity

time (s)

STOPPING DISTANCES

A car which is travelling at a constant velocity is experiencing balanced forces. In order to slow down and stop the retarding or deceleration forces need to be greater than the propulsive forces. This is achieved in two ways:

- The driver removes his foot from the accelerator to reduce the force from the engine driving the car forward.

- he applies the brakes which increases the friction between the road and the car's tyres.

The minimum distance a car will travel before coming to a halt after the brakes have been applied will depend upon:

- thinking time (the reaction time of the driver)

- the surface conditions of the road and the tyres

- the speed of the car immediately prior to braking

Shortest stopping distances on a dry road		
At 13 m/s (30 mph)		
thinking distance 9 m	braking distance 14 m	total stopping distance 23 m
At 22 m/s (50 mph)		
thinking distance 15 m	braking distance 38 m	total stopping distance 53 m
At 30 m/s (70 mph)		
thinking distance 21 m	braking distance 75 m	total stopping distance 96 m
The distances shown in car length are based on an average family car		

C11 Moments

MOMENTS

Sometimes when a force is applied to an object it may cause it to turn or twist.

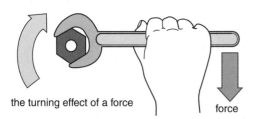

the turning effect of a force   force

This turning effect of a force is called a **moment**.
The size of a moment depends upon the size of the force and where it is applied.

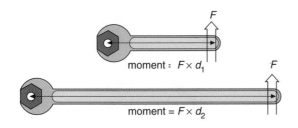

moment = $F \times d_1$

moment = $F \times d_2$

moment of a force	= applied force ×	perpendicular distance of force from fulcrum

moment = $F \times d$

Undoing a stiff nut with a long spanner is much easier than using a short one because of the larger moment it creates.

Pedalling uphill is much easier if the large cog on the rear wheel is used as the force transmitted through the chain can create a larger moment.

PRINCIPLE OF MOMENTS

In Indian wrestling both contestants try to create a moment which is so large that it overpowers their opponent causing both arms to pivot around the elbows.

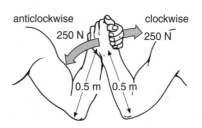

anticlockwise   250 N   clockwise   250 N

0.5 m   0.5 m

In the early stages of such a contest there is often no movement ie there is **equilibrium** or balance. This is because the *clockwise moments* and the *anticlockwise* moments are equal.

Similarly if an object such as a see-saw is balanced (in equilibrium) then the sum of the clockwise moments must be equal to the sum of the anticlockwise moments.

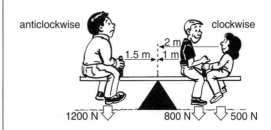

anticlockwise   clockwise
2 m
1.5 m   1 m
1200 N   800 N   500 N

Anticlockwise moment = 1200 N × 1.5 m

= 1800 Nm

Clockwise moments = 500 N × 2 m + 800 N × 1 m

= 1800 Nm

SIMPLE LEVERS

To lift this rock unaided would require a force of 500 N. However, if a lever is used much less effort (force) is needed.

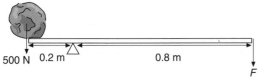

500 N

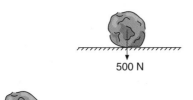

500 N   0.2 m   0.8 m

F

At the point at which the rock is just about to move the clockwise moments and the anticlockwise moments must be equal.

Clockwise moment = anticlockwise moment

$$F \times 0.8 \text{ m} = 500 \text{ N} \times 0.2 \text{ m}$$

$$F = \frac{500 \text{ N} \times 0.2 \text{ m}}{0.8 \text{ m}}$$

$$F = 125 \text{ N}$$

Moving large amounts of earth around the garden can be hard work. Using a wheelbarrow makes the task much easier. To lift a load before the wheelbarrow is pushed the gardener needs to create a moment equal to that created by the soil.

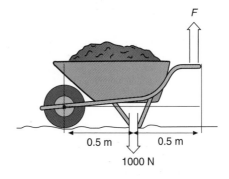

F

0.5 m   0.5 m

1000 N

Using the principle of moments:

clockwise moment = anticlockwise moment

$$F \times 1.0 \text{ m} = 1000 \text{ N} \times 0.5 \text{ m}$$

$$F = 500 \text{ N}$$

C12 Stability

CENTRE OF MASS (GRAVITY)

This high jumper has to do work in order to lift his body over the bar. The amount of work can be calculated using:

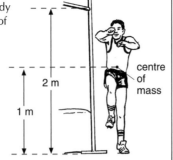

2 m

1 m

jumper's weight 750 N

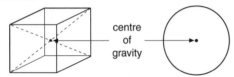

work done = force × distance moved

The average force they will need to apply will be approximately equal to their weight in newtons but through what distance must this weight be moved? The jumper's weight is obviously spread throughout their body. To overcome this problem it is imagined that all the weight of the jumper is concentrated in one place called the **centre of mass** or **centre of gravity**. The position of the centre of mass of any object depends upon its shape and how its mass is distributed.

centre of gravity

The centre of mass of a regularly shaped object is often at its geometric centre.

The centre of mass of an irregular shaped object can be found by hanging the object from a pin on a stand so that it is free to swing. A vertical line is then drawn through the pivot (pin) using a plumb line. The object is then suspended from a different position and a second vertical line drawn. The centre of mass is located where the two lines cross. If an object is supported directly beneath its centre of mass it will balance as there are no moments causing it to topple.

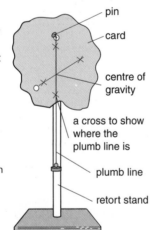

pin

card

centre of gravity

a cross to show where the plumb line is

plumb line

retort stand

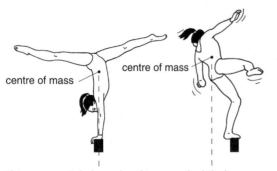

centre of mass

centre of mass

This gymnast is balanced and in control whilst her centre of mass is directly above the beam. If however her centre of mass is slightly to one side her weight creates a moment causing her to topple.

STABILITY

When racing cars are designed, a great deal of care is taken to ensure that they are **stable** so they are unlikely to turn over. To achieve this modern racing cars have a wide wheel base and a low centre of mass.

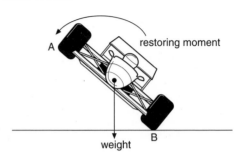

restoring moment

A

B

weight

Stable objects can be tilted through quite a large angle and when released they return to their original position. This happens because a vertical line from the centre of mass still lies inside AB. The weight creates a restoring moment.

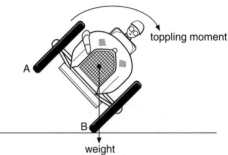

toppling moment

A

B

weight

Older racing cars were not so well designed ... because they were narrower and had a higher centre of mass they were unstable. When tilted just a little the vertical line from the centre of mass falls outside the base AB. Now the weight of the car creates a moment causing it to topple over.

Examples of stable and unstable objects

Some objects when they are tilted and then released neither return to their original position nor fall over. They stay where they are tilted. These objects are said to have neutral stability. Their centre of mass is always directly above their base.

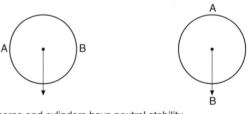

A

B

A

B

Spheres and cylinders have neutral stability.

D1 Pressure

PRINCIPLE OF PRESSURE

If a force is applied to an object its effect will often depend upon how it is concentrated. Pressure is a measure of the concentration or distribution of a force applied.

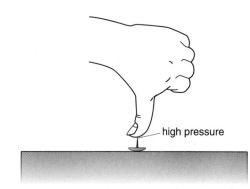
high pressure

The two Inuit people above are the same weight. The one on the left however is wearing snow shoes. His weight, therefore is spread over a larger area and creates less pressure than that of his friend. Consequently, although his friend sinks into the snow, he does not.

With the drawing pin upside down, the applied force would create a high pressure on the pad of the thumb. With the pin the correct way round the force is spread on the head of the pin directly under the thumb but is concentrated at the point at the surface of the pinboard.

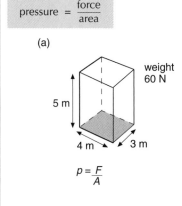

DO NOT TRY THIS YOURSELF

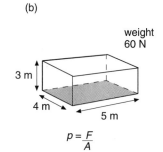

By using a ladder to spread his weight over a large surface area this rescuer avoids applying a large pressure to the ice.

The more nails this fakir has in his bed the happier he is!!!!! As the number of nails increases so too does the surface area over which his weight is distributed. Hence the lower the pressure applied to his skin by each nail.

CALCULATING PRESSURE

The pressure created by a force can be calculated using the equation

$$\text{pressure} = \frac{\text{force}}{\text{area}}$$

Pressure is measured in **pascals** (**Pa**) where $1\ \text{Pa} = 1\ \text{N/m}^2$

If a heavy box is placed on a table the pressure exerted by the box would depend upon which face it stands on.

(a)

weight 60 N

5 m

4 m   3 m

$p = \dfrac{F}{A}$

$p = \dfrac{60\ \text{N}}{12\ \text{m}^2}$

$p = 5\ \text{Pa}$

(b)

weight 60 N

3 m

4 m

5 m

$p = \dfrac{F}{A}$

$p = \dfrac{60\ \text{N}}{20\ \text{m}^2}$

$p = 3\ \text{Pa}$

(c)

weight 60 N

4 m

3 m   5 m

$p = \dfrac{F}{A}$

$p = \dfrac{60\ \text{N}}{15\ \text{m}^2}$

$p = 4\ \text{Pa}$

D2 Pressure in fluids

PRESSURE IN LIQUIDS

This diver is experiencing the pressure which is being exerted by the surrounding liquid. The size of the pressure depends upon:

- the depth of the liquid
- the density of the liquid

In simple terms the pressure experienced is due to the weight of liquid above.

Water from this container rushes out of the holes at different rates depending upon the pressure in the liquid. The experiment clearly confirms that:

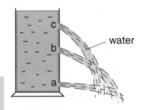

water

> **In a liquid pressure increases with depth.**
>
> $P_a > P_b > P_c$

If an inflated spherical balloon is taken deep below the surface of the sea it would shrink in size the deeper it was taken.

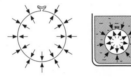

In the laboratory this can be demonstrated using this apparatus. The liquid gushes out of all of the holes at the same rate in every direction.

pressure in the liquid is the same in all directions

water   can

Hydraulic Jack

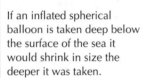

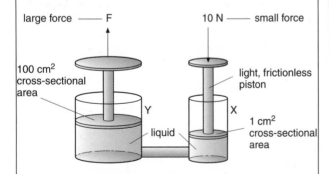

large force —— F   10 N —— small force

100 cm² cross-sectional area

light, frictionless piston

Y   X

liquid   1 cm² cross-sectional area

Liquids are **incompressible**. They cannot be squashed. If a force of 10 N is applied through piston X it will create a pressure of 10 N/cm² throughout the liquid.

At Z the pressure in the liquid must still be 10 Ncm². If the cross-sectional area of piston Y is 100 times greater than that of piston X, the force applied upwards from the liquid must be 100 times greater (1000 N). So a small force applied at X has resulted in a much larger force being applied at Y. This is the principle behind the hydraulic jack.

PRESSURE IN GASES

Gases like liquids exert pressure on any object which is immersed in them.

Air molecules (which move at approximately 400–500 m/s) create **atmospheric pressure**.

Effects of atmospheric pressure

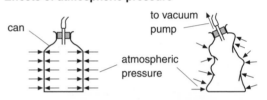

can

to vacuum pump

atmospheric pressure

Before the air is withdrawn from this can the pressure inside and outside are equal and balanced. When the air is removed the atmospheric pressure outside is sufficiently large to crush the can.

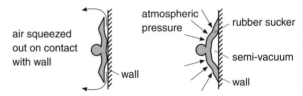

air squeezed out on contact with wall

atmospheric pressure   rubber sucker

semi-vacuum

wall   wall

When a sucker is pushed onto a surface the air inside is squeezed out. When released, the sucker is held against the surface by atmospheric pressure.

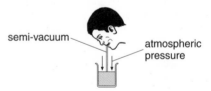

semi-vacuum   atmospheric pressure

When air is sucked out of a straw there is a decrease in pressure which allows the larger atmospheric pressure to push the liquid up the straw.

Aneroid barometer

Atmospheric pressure can be used to predict changes in the weather. If atmospheric pressure increases, the corrugated box is squeezed a little which causes the pointer to move. If the pressure decreases the box expands and the pointer moves the opposite way.

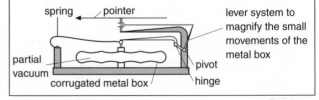

spring   pointer

lever system to magnify the small movements of the metal box

partial vacuum

corrugated metal box   pivot   hinge

E1 Wave properties (1)

WAVE MOTION

A wave is a means of moving energy from place to place but without any transfer of matter. Here on the Earth, animals and plants receive over 99% of their energy through light waves from the Sun.

There are two main groups of waves.

> There are **transverse** waves and **longitudinal** waves.

A transverse wave is one in which the vibrations (oscillations) are at right angles to the direction in which the wave (energy) is moving. Examples of transverse waves include water waves, light waves, and some mechanical waves like the one shown below.

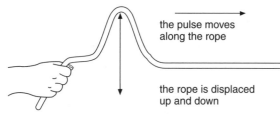

the pulse moves along the rope

the rope is displaced up and down

If a series of regular pulses is sent along the rope the wave will look like this:

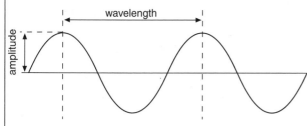

The maximum displacement of the rope is called the **amplitude** of the wave. The distance between two successive peaks is called the **wavelength**.

All waves begin with vibrations. The object producing the wave vibrates at a rate called the **frequency** of the wave and is measured in Hertz (Hz). A wave has a frequency of 50 Hz if 50 complete waves are produced by the vibrating object each second. The **period** of a wave (T) is the time it takes the *vibrating* object to produce one full wave.

A longitudinal wave is one in which the vibrations are along the direction in which the wave is moving. Examples of longitudinal waves include sound waves, and some mechanical waves like the one shown below.

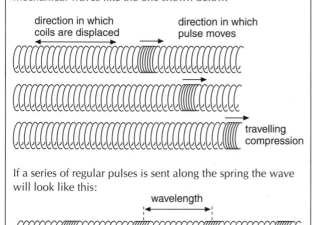

direction in which coils are displaced

direction in which pulse moves

travelling compression

If a series of regular pulses is sent along the spring the wave will look like this:

wavelength

compression   rarefaction   compression

THE RIPPLE TANK

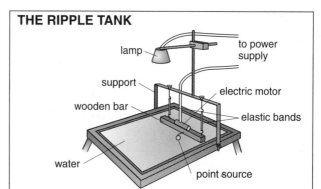

lamp — to power supply — support — electric motor — wooden bar — elastic bands — water — point source

One of the most convenient ways to study the basic properties of waves is to use a *ripple tank*. When the small electric motor is turned on the wooden bar vibrates creating a series of ripples in the tank. Shadows of these ripples can be cast onto a white sheet making the movement of the waves easy to see.

Plane and point sources

A vibrating point source will produce circular wavefronts

A vibrating plane source will produce plane wavefronts

Frequency and wavelength

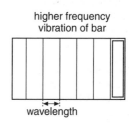

low frequency vibration of bar

higher frequency vibration of bar

wavelength   wavelength

The lower the frequency of the source, the longer the wavelength of the waves produced.

WAVE EQUATION

The relationship between the frequency (f) and the period (T) of a wave is given by:

> frequency (Hz) = $\dfrac{1}{\text{period (s)}}$

> $f = \dfrac{1}{T}$

The relationship between velocity (v), frequency (f) and wavelength (λ) of all waves are given by:

> $v = f \lambda$

Example

If the speed of sound is 340 m/s calculate the wavelength of a note whose frequency is 170 Hz.

Using:

$$v = f \lambda$$
$$340 \text{ m/s} = 170 \text{ Hz} \times \lambda$$
$$\lambda = \frac{340 \text{ m/s}}{170 \text{ Hz}}$$
$$\lambda = 2 \text{ m}$$

E2 Wave properties (2)

REFLECTION FROM PLANE AND CURVED SURFACES

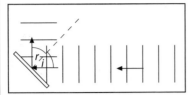

waves which strike a plane barrier will be reflected such that angle *i* = angle *r*

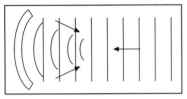

waves which strike a concave barrier will converge

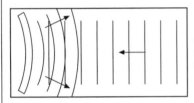

waves which strike a convex barrier will diverge

INTERFERENCE

If two dippers are connected to the vibrating wooden bar in a ripple tank each will produce its own circular wave pattern. Where the two patterns overlap they combine or **interfere** to produce an **interference pattern**.

overlapping waves

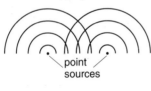

point sources

resulting interference pattern.

In those places where the waves interfere **constructively**, a new wave of larger amplitude is created.

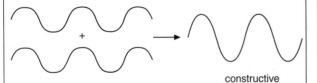

constructive interference

In those places where the waves interfere **destructively**, a wave of smaller amplitude (or no amplitude) is created.

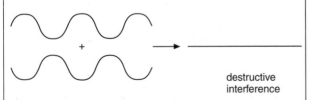

destructive interference

REFRACTION

It is possible to change the direction of a wave by altering the medium through which it is travelling. With water waves this is achieved by changing the depth of the water.

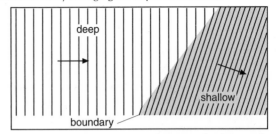

deep

shallow

boundary

As the waves cross the boundary between the deep and shallower water the change in velocity causes them to change direction or **refract**.

DIFFRACTION

The spreading of waves at the edges of objects or as they pass through a narrow gap is called **diffraction**.

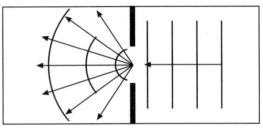

If the gap is similar in size to the wavelength of the waves the diffraction is large.

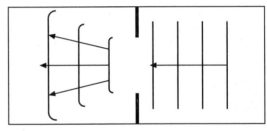

If the is much larger or much smaller than the wavelength of the waves the diffraction is much less.

Often before a harbour is built a scale model is placed inside a ripple tank in order to discover to what extent the proposed harbour entrance is likely to diffract waves.

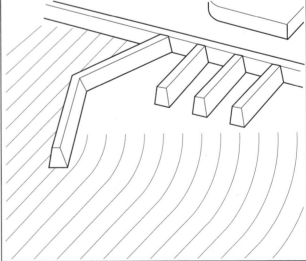

E3 Sound (1)

Origins of sound

All sounds begin with an object vibrating: the strings of a guitar; the skin of a drum; the reed of a clarinet. If the object is large, such as a double bass, the strings will vibrate slowly and produce a low-pitched note. If the object is small, such as a violin, the strings will vibrate quickly and produce a high-pitched note.

large musical instruments produce low-pitched notes

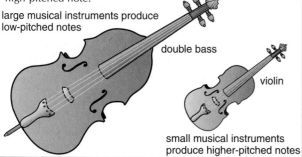

double bass

violin

small musical instruments produce higher-pitched notes

SOUND WAVES

As an object vibrates back and forth it pushes the air particles immediately next to it, creating a series of compressions and rarefactions. This moving chain of compressions and rarefactions is a sound wave.

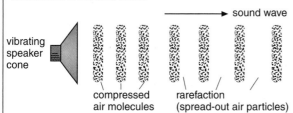

sound wave

vibrating speaker cone

compressed air molecules

rarefaction (spread-out air particles)

Sound waves can travel through solids, liquids, or gases. They can travel through any medium providing there are particles present. If the particles are close together, as they are in solids and liquids, sound waves will pass through them very easily and quickly.

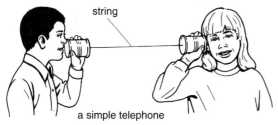

string

a simple telephone

Quietly spoken words travelling as sound waves through the air cannot be easily heard because the gas particles are spread out and so cannot easily pass on the vibrations.

Those same words can however be heard much more clearly through the vibrations in the string.

If there are no particles there is no means by which the vibrations can be passed on. *Sound cannot travel through a vacuum.*

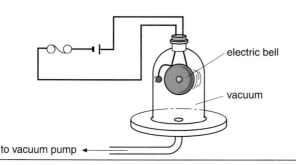

electric bell

vacuum

to vacuum pump

PITCH, LOUDNESS

Although it is not possible to see sound waves directly an instrument called a *cathode ray oscilloscope* (CRO) can be used to show those features of a wave that correspond to pitch, loudness, and tone.

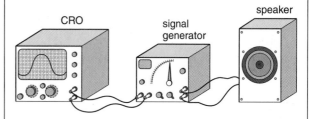

CRO

signal generator

speaker

Pitch

The pitch of a note is related to the frequency of the vibration. The higher the pitch the higher the frequency.

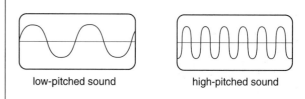

low-pitched sound

high-pitched sound

Loudness

The loudness or amplitude of a note depends upon the number of air particles hitting an eardrum at a particular time. The more particles that do this the louder the note. A loud note is seen on the CRO as a tall wave, ie the wave has a large **amplitude**.

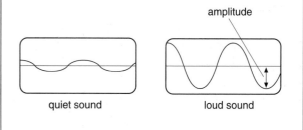

amplitude

quiet sound

loud sound

DECIBEL SCALE

The loudness of a sound is measured in decibels (dB).

Decibels dB	Sound
0	absolute quiet
30	small bird singing
50	normal conversation
90	someone shouting close by
100	road works using heavy machinery
120	close to the stage at a rock concert. Persistent exposure to noise of this level will lead to permanent damage to one's eardrums.
140	standing within 50 m of a commercial aircraft as it is about to take off. At this level the sound will cause pain and possibly nausea.

E4 Sound (2)

ECHOES

Ships often use echoes ... **SONAR** (**SO**und **N**avigation **A**nd **R**anging) ... to discover how deep the ocean is beneath them or to detect shoals of fish. The ship emits a sound wave which is reflected from any object below. The time lapse before the echo is detected indicates the depth of the object.

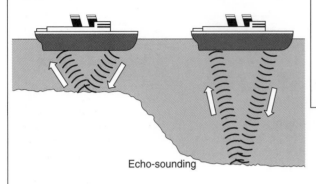

Echo-sounding

Ultrasound echoes

Bats use echoes in order to avoid flying into objects and to detect their prey. The sounds used by bats have frequencies greater than 20 000 Hz and are beyond the human hearing range (20 ... 20 000 Hz). They are called **ultrasounds**.

Ultrasounds can be extremely useful:

- in industry for cleaning and quality control
  Because ultrasounds have such high frequencies their vibrations can be used to shake dirt from surfaces that need to be clean (even our teeth)

- to detect flaws and cracks within pieces of metal. These flaws would go unnoticed with just a visual inspection.

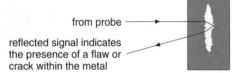

from probe →

reflected signal indicates
the presence of a flaw or
crack within the metal

SPEED OF SOUND

The speed of sound at sea level is approximately 340 m/s. The speed of light is much, much quicker ie 3×10^8 m/s. This is why an event is often seen before it is heard. The flash of lightning is seen before the thunder is heard, the cricketer is seen to hit the ball before the stroke is heard.

The speed of sound can then be calculated using the equation

$$\text{speed} = \frac{\text{distance travelled}}{\text{time taken}}$$

Anything which travels faster than the speed of sound is described as being **supersonic**.

- in medicine for pre-natal scanning.

An ultrasonic scanner sends pulses of ultrasound into the patient's body. At the boundary between different types of tissue eg muscle and bone the waves are reflected. These echoes are then processed by a computer to create an image on a screen. Using this technique for monitoring the growth of a baby in the mother's womb is ideal as it presents no threat to their health. X-rays cannot be used as they might affect the unborn baby.

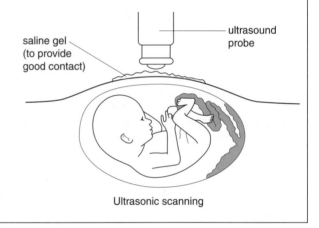

saline gel
(to provide
good contact)

ultrasound
probe

Ultrasonic scanning

SEISMIC WAVES

There are two main types of shock waves associated with earthquakes. These are:
- P (primary) waves which are fast-moving longitudinal waves. As these waves reach the surface the rocks there are stretched and compressed which causes the ground to shudder up and down.

- S (secondary) waves which are slower-moving transverse waves. When these waves reach the surface the rocks are made to shake or vibrate from side to side.

As the P and S waves travel at different speeds there is a time delay between their arrival at the surface. The length of this delay provides information about how far away the source of the earthquake (epicentre) is.

Structure of the Earth

Much of the knowledge about the structure of the Earth comes from the study of shockwaves (**seismology**). As the P and S waves travel through the Earth they encounter regions and rocks of different densities which cause the waves to change direction. Small changes in density cause the waves to curve or change direction gradually. Large changes in density eg between different types of rock cause the waves to change direction abruptly. Also, P waves travel through liquids and solids whilst S waves can only travel through solids.

Observations of the paths of these waves suggest that the Earth's structure is that shown below.

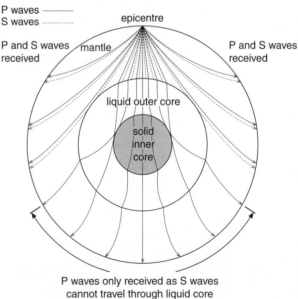

P waves ————
S waves ··········

epicentre

P and S waves
received

mantle

P and S waves
received

liquid outer core

solid
inner
core

P waves only received as S waves
cannot travel through liquid core

Paths of seismic waves through the Earth

E5 Reflection of light

LIGHT RAYS

We see **luminous** objects such as the Sun, light bulbs, and candle flames because of the light they *emit*. We see **non-luminous** objects such as the Moon, trees, and other people because of the light rays they *reflect*. If there is no source of light we cannot see.

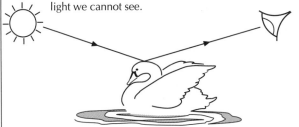

REFLECTIONS

Reflection from a plane mirror

When a ray of light strikes a plane mirror it is reflected such that the angle of incidence (*i*) is equal to the angle of reflection (*r*).

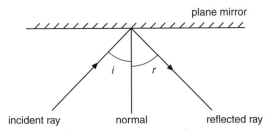

Plane and diffuse reflection

When parallel rays of light strike an object which has a smooth surface the rays are all reflected in the same direction (angle *i* = angle *r*). The surface of the object therefore looks shiny.

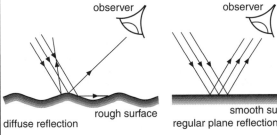

diffuse reflection   rough surface   smooth surface   regular plane reflection

When parallel rays of light strike an object which has a rough surface they are reflected in many different directions. So to an observer the surface of the object appears dull. Shoes are shiny after polishing because the polish fills in the rough surface of the leather making it smooth.

Image in a plane mirror.

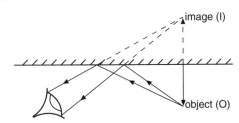

The diagram above shows how the image (I) of an object (O) is created by a plane mirror. The brain of the observer believes that light travels in straight lines and that the rays of light therefore have come from the image (I). It sees an image of the object behind the mirror.

SHADOWS

Transparent objects allow light to pass through them.
Opaque objects do not allow light to pass through them.

If an opaque object is placed in the path of light from a point source a uniformly dark shadow (**umbra**) is created.

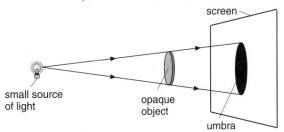

If an extended or larger light source is used the shadow is not uniformly dark. In those areas on the screen where the light is only partly blocked out a lighter shadow (**penumbra**) is created.

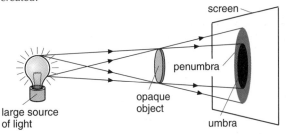

During a *solar eclipse* both umbra and penumbra are created. The umbra is the result of a total eclipse, whilst the penumbra is the result of a partial eclipse.

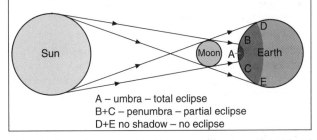

A – umbra – total eclipse
B+C – penumbra – partial eclipse
D+E no shadow – no eclipse

The image (I) is called a **virtual** image as rays of light do not actually pass through it. Images through which rays of light actually pass are known as **real** images. Real images like those from a projector can be put onto a screen, virtual images like those created by a plane mirror cannot be put onto a screen.

The image created by a plane mirror is always
- the same size as the object
- the same distance behind the mirror as the object is in front
- upright
- laterally inverted (ie right to left and left to right)
- virtual

Simple periscope

Some optical instruments like the simple periscope use plane mirrors to change the direction of rays of light. In this case it is possible to see over an obstacle using a periscope.

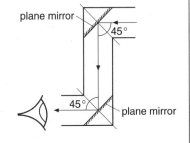

E6 Refraction of light

Light travels through a vacuum at a speed of 3×10^8 m/s. In other media such as water or glass, it travels at different speeds. This change in speed as light enters or leaves media of different densities is called **refraction**. Refraction results in the rays of light changing direction as they cross the boundary between the media.

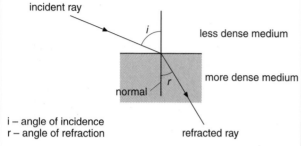

i – angle of incidence
r – angle of refraction

> As a ray of light travels from a less dense medium to a more dense medium it bends towards the *normal*.

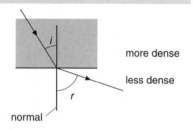

> As a ray of light travels from a more dense medium to a less dense medium it bends away from the *normal*.

However, if the ray of light crosses the boundary at 90° it continues on in a straight line. It is undeviated.

Why does a ray of light bend when it crosses the boundary between two media?

Below, a ray of light of width AB travels from air into a more dense medium (such as glass).

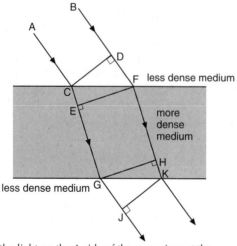

When the light on the A side of the ray arrives at the boundary it travels more slowly. The B side of the ray has still not reached the boundary and therefore continues at its higher speed. The effect of this is that the ray changes direction (turns slightly clockwise) towards the normal. Inside the block all parts of the ray are travelling at the same speed so it continues in a straight line. On reaching the second boundary the A side of the ray is the first to leave the glass and speeds up. The effect of this is that the ray again changes direction, this time bending away from the normal.

EFFECTS OF REFRACTION.

If you look at the bottom of a swimming pool from above the the water, or you look at a pencil which is half immersed in water you can observe some of the everyday effects of refraction.

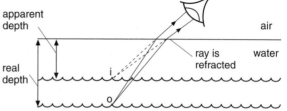

When the rays of light from the bottom of the pool cross the water/air boundary they speed up and bend away from the normal. The eye of the observer does not realise this and sees the rays as having come from I instead of from O. The water appears much shallower than it really is.

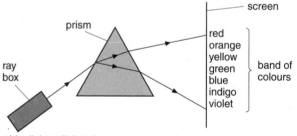

a pencil appears bent when immersed in water

In the case of the pencil refraction will make the pencil look as if it is bent.

DISPERSION OF WHITE LIGHT

When white light passes through a prism it emerges as a band of colours called a **spectrum**. This effect is called **dispersion** and occurs because white light is a mixture of colours. At each of the two surfaces of the prism the colours are refracted by different amounts. The longer wavelengths (red, orange ...) are refracted the least. The shorter wavelengths (indigo and violet) are refracted the most.

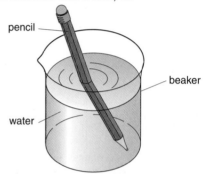

white light split into its components using a prism

A second identical prism can be used to recombine the colours to again produce white light.

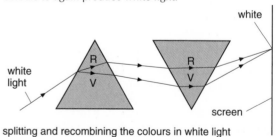

splitting and recombining the colours in white light

E7 Total internal reflection

Sometimes when a ray of light is about to cross the boundary between an (optically) more dense and an (optically) less dense medium the ray is reflected rather than refracted ie the surface acts as if it were a mirror. This phenomenon is called **total internal reflection**.

For total internal reflection to take place:
- the ray must be travelling from a more dense medium to a less dense medium
- the ray must strike the boundary at an angle greater than the **critical angle**.

If the angle is less than the critical angle the ray is refracted.

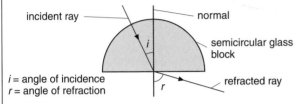

i = angle of incidence
r = angle of refraction

If the angle is greater than the critical angle total internal reflection takes place.

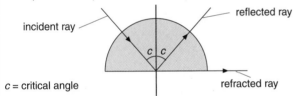

i = angle of incidence
r_i = angle of reflection
$i = r_i$

The angle which is the boundary between these two conditions is called the *critical angle*.

At the critical angle grazing emergence should occur, although often part of the ray is refracted whilst part of it is reflected.

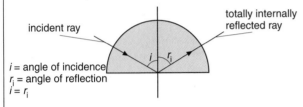

c = critical angle

Different materials have different critical angles
eg   glass 42.0°, water 49.0°, perspex 42.2°, alcohol 47.3°

PRISMS

Prism shaped pieces of glass or plastic are often used to reflect light because they do it far more efficiently than mirrors. They reflect more of the light and so produce a brighter image and also they are less fragile.

Prismatic periscope

Light from the object enters prism A normally and so strikes the inner surface at 45°. This is greater than the critical angle for glass so the ray undergoes total internal reflection turning through 90°. At prism B the ray is again turned through 90°.

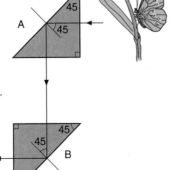

Using total internal refraction in a prismatic telescope

Bicycle reflectors and cat's eyes

Bicycle reflectors and cat's eyes are designed to reflect light back in the direction from which it came. They achieve this by using the ability of prisms to reflect light.

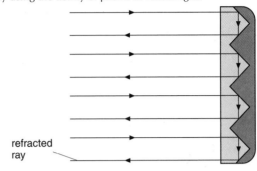

a bicycle reflector

The light from the source strikes two of the surfaces at 45° and so is turned overall through 180° – back in the direction from which it came.

Prismatic binoculars

Binoculars are much more compact than telescopes as they use prisms to reflect the light back and forth.

Optical fibres

Optic fibres are designed to conduct or pipe rays of light along their length. Light which enters a fibre at one end is unable to escape as it undergoes a whole series of total internal reflections until it emerges at the far end. Even when a fibre is bent the light remains trapped inside. Light can be made to 'travel round corners'.

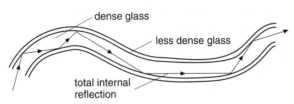

The importance of being able to do this has been demonstrated with the recent development of keyhole surgery. If several thousand optic fibres are tied together to make a bundle this flexible light pipe allows doctors to see inside parts of the body which previously would have required a major exploratory operation. A similar device is used by engineers to inspect those parts of a machine or structure which are not normally readily accessible.

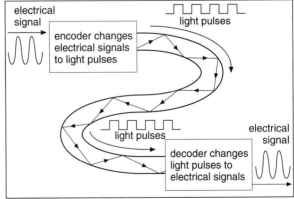

Optical fibres are also used in telecommunications. They are replacing the much more expensive and heavier copper cables. Also, the fibres are capable of carrying far more signals.

E8 Lenses

A lens is a specially shaped piece of glass or plastic which refracts light in a predictable and useful way. There are two main types of lens: **convex** and **concave**.

Convex or converging lenses
A convex lens is shaped so that rays of light which pass through it are brought together or converge. The fatter the lens the shorter the *focal length* (*f*) and the more quickly the rays are made to converge. The *focal point* (*F*) of a convex lens is the point to which rays of light travelling parallel to the principal axis converge after refraction.

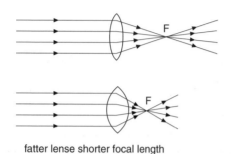

fatter lense shorter focal length

Concave or diverging lenses.
A concave lens is shaped so that rays of light which pass through it are made to diverge.

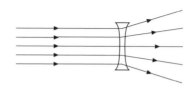

Main parts of a lens

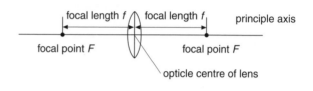

RAY DIAGRAMS
Convex lenses
For a convex lens there are three rays of light which pass through the lens in a predictable manner:

- a ray of light travelling parallel to the principal axis will, on being refracted by a convex lens, pass through its focal point.

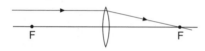

- a ray of light which passes through the focal point of a convex lens will, on being refracted by a convex lens, travel parallel to the principal axis.

- a ray of light which passes through the optical centre of the lens will be undeviated.

Ray diagrams can be used to show how a convex lens can produce different kinds of images – real, virtual, magnified, and diminished.

Object placed between F and 2F

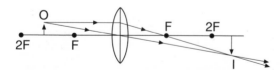

This is the arrangement used in a slide projector where the projection lens forms a real, inverted, magnified image of a slide on a screen.

Object placed beyond 2F

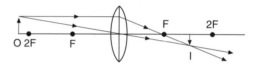

This is the arrangement used in a camera and in the eye. The image is real, diminished, and inverted.

Object placed between F and the lens

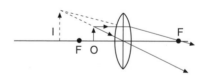

The image created is magnified, virtual, the same side of the lens as the object, and is upright. This diagram shows how a convex lens can be used as a magnifying glass.

Concave lenses
For a concave lens:
- a ray travelling parallel to the principal axis is refracted so that it appears to have come from the focal point.

- a ray travelling through the centre of the lens is undeviated.

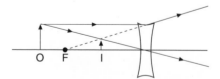

The image created by a concave lens is always upright, diminished and virtual.

E9 Optical instruments (1)

PINHOLE CAMERA

The pinhole camera consists a light-proof box with a single small pinhole in one side. Rays of light from an object enter the box creating an image of the object on the far side.

The image which is created is:
- dim
- real
- upside down
- always sharp

Although the image created by a pinhole camera is always in focus (sharp) it is also very dim. If the pinhole is made larger in order to allow more light to enter the image becomes blurred.

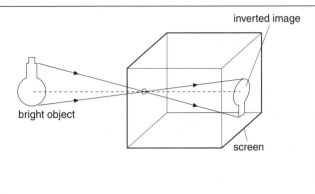

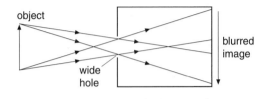

MODERN CAMERA

Light from an object enters the camera through a small hole called the *aperture*. The size of the aperture can be altered to let in more or less light depending upon the conditions. The light entering the camera is refracted by a lens which focuses the light onto the film, creating a sharp image. The images of objects at different distances from the camera are brought to focus by altering the distance between the lens and the film.

To obtain the correct exposure for the film the amount of light entering the camera must be controlled. This can be done by altering the size of the aperture or by adjusting the time the shutter allows the light to reach the film.

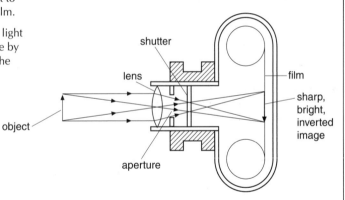

PROJECTOR

Light is concentrated from the lamp onto the slide by the concave mirror and the condenser lenses. A magnified inverted image of the strongly illuminated slide is then projected on the screen by the convex projection lens. The distance between the projection lens and the slide can be altered in order to focus the image on the screen.

The image is:
- inverted
- in focus
- real
- bright
- magnified

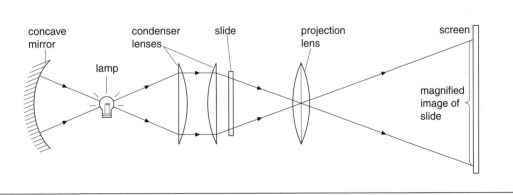

E10 Optical instruments (2)

THE EYE

Light enters the eye through the cornea. It then travels through the aqueous humour and the pupil until it reaches the eye lens. Here it is refracted in order to produce a sharp image on the retina. The retina then sends electrical messages along the optic nerve to the brain which processes these signals so that an upright clear image is seen.

Cornea - This is a clear, hard covering which protects the front of the eye. Because its surface is curved it also does most of the focusing of the rays.

Aqueous humour and vitreous humour - Two transparent liquids that help to keep the shape of the eye round.

Pupil - The hole or window through which light travels to reach the eye lens.

Iris - The coloured part of the eye which controls how much light reaches the retina. If too much light is entering the eye the iris reduces the size of the pupil. If too little light is entering the eye the pupil dilates ie it becomes bigger.

Eye lens - The shape of the eye lens (ie its focal length) can be altered so that sharp images of near and far objects can be created on the retina. This process is called **accommodation**.

Ciliary muscles - If we look at a near object the rays of light need to be refracted quite a lot in order to produce a sharp image. To achieve this the ciliary muscles contract, altering the shape of the eye lens, making it shorter and fatter. If we look at a distant object the rays need to be refracted just a little. To achieve this the ciliary muscles relax making the lens long and thin.

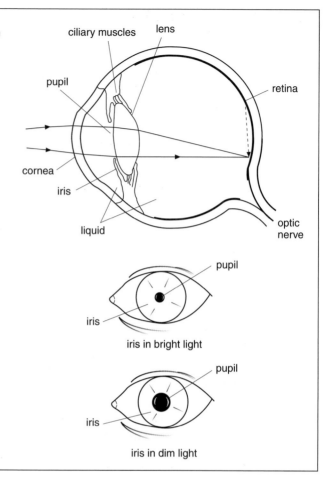

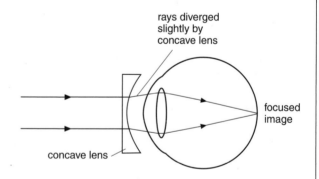

iris in bright light

iris in dim light

EYE DEFECTS

People who can see near objects but cannot see distant objects clearly are said to be **short-sighted**. This occurs because the eye lens focuses the rays in front of the retina, creating a blurred image.

This problem can be overcome by wearing concave glasses or contact lenses.

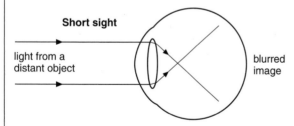

Short sight

light from a distant object

blurred image

rays diverged slightly by concave lens

concave lens

focused image

People who can see distant objects but cannot see near objects are said to be **long-sighted**. This occurs because the eye lens focuses the rays of light behind the retina.

This problem is overcome by wearing convex glasses or contact lenses.

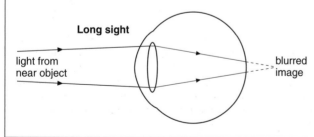

Long sight

light from near object

blurred image

rays converged slightly by convex lens

convex lens

focused image

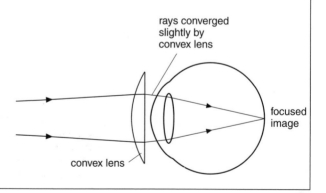

E11 The electromagnetic spectrum (1)

ELECTROMAGNETIC WAVES

Visible light is just one small part of the **electromagnetic spectrum**.

All electromagnetic waves:

- transfer energy from place to place

- travel in a vacuum at the 'speed of light' 3×10^8 m/s

- are transverse waves and can be *polarised*

- exhibit basic wave properties. (They can be reflected, refracted, diffracted, and create interference patterns.)

The properties of the groups of waves within the electromagnetic spectrum vary because of their different frequencies and wavelengths.

The diagram below summarises the most important features of the different regions of the spectrum.

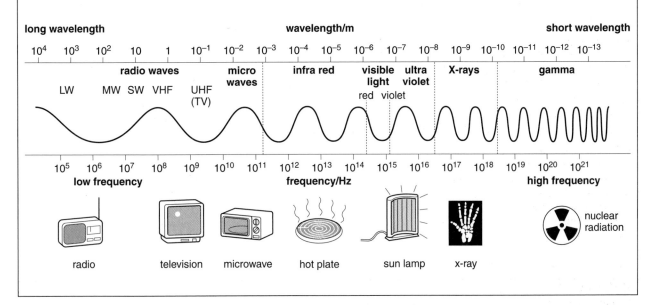

GAMMA RAYS

Gamma rays are high frequency rays emitted from some radioactive materials.

They:
- are highly penetrating and can easily pass through body tissue

- can damage living cells, possibly causing cancer

- can with closely monitored dosages be used to treat/kill certain types of cancer (radiotherapy)

- can be used to kill micro-organisms in food so that it will keep for longer (irradiation)

- can be used to irradiate surgical instruments to sterilise them

X-RAYS

X-rays are produced when fast moving electrons strike a metal plate such as tungsten.

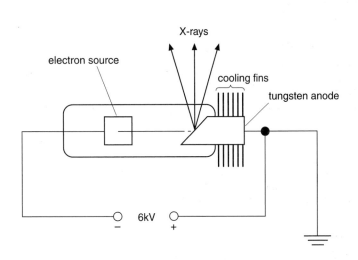

They penetrate certain parts of the body such as tissue but not bone or teeth, and so are used to produce shadow pictures in order to detect faults such as breakages or cracks. X-rays can be dangerous: over exposure to X-rays can harm certain parts of the body such as sex organs. To avoid this operators of X-ray machines in hospitals and industry stand behind a lead screen which shields them from accidental exposure to the X-rays.

E12 The elecromagnetic spectrum (2)

ULTRAVIOLET RAYS

It is the ultraviolet rays from the Sun which cause tanning and produce vitamin D in our skin but over-exposure to ultraviolet can cause skin cancer.

When they are exposed to ultraviolet some chemicals **fluoresce** – they emit visible light when invisible ultraviolet light is shone on them. These chemicals are used in:

- security paints and markers
- washing powders so that clothes will appear 'whiter than white' when exposed to sunlight

VISIBLE LIGHT

This is the only part of the electromagnetic spectrum which can be seen by the eye. Light of different frequencies is seen as different colours.

If all the colours of the visible spectrum are mixed together they produce white light.

red
+
orange
+
yellow
+
green   } = white
+
blue
+
indigo
+
violet

Coloured objects

When exposed to white light a red object looks red. This is reflected into the observer's eye. Blue and green objects behave in a similar way reflecting blue and green light respectively.

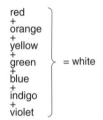

red T-shirt

white light

reflected red light

observer

The red T-shirt reflects only red light

When exposed to white light a white object looks white because it reflects all colours.

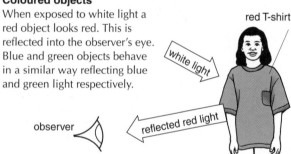

white light

reflected white light

observer

The white T-shirt reflects all the different colours.

When exposed to white light a black object looks black because it absorbs all colours so none are reflected.

white light

observer

The black T-shirt reflects no light

INFRARED RAYS

Anything which is warm gives off infrared rays. It is not normally possible to see it with our eyes but we can feel it as heat radiation. The infrared radiation feels warm as it stimulates the nerves in our skin. Some animals such as rattle snakes have very sensitive infrared sensors which they use to detect the warm bodies of their prey.

Special photographic film and thermal intensifiers use infrared to allow us to 'see in the dark'.

Remote control keypads for TVs, videos and stereo systems all use infrared rays for controlling programmes.

MICROWAVES

Microwaves are produced in very high frequency electrical circuits. In a microwave oven water molecules inside the food absorb energy and become hot. In this way heating (cooking) occurs throughout the food.

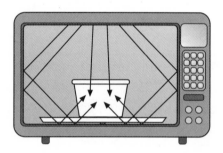

If microwaves strike a metallic object they are reflected. This is the principle behind radar which is used to detect and plot the movement of aircraft, ships, and cars. **RADAR** stands for **RA**dio **D**etection **A**nd **R**anging.

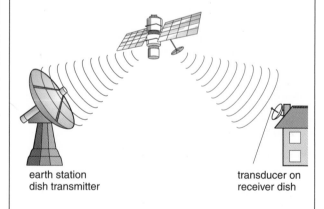

earth station
dish transmitter

transducer on
receiver dish

Microwaves are also used for national and international communication systems. Signals are sent in the form of microwaves to ground stations. From there they are beamed via large dish aerials to geostationary satellites above the Earth. The satellites amplify the signals and redirect them to other ground stations.

RADIO WAVES

Radio waves have the largest wavelength in the electromagnetic spectrum. One of their main uses is to carry messages and signals over large distance ie communications.

F1 Static electricity

POSITIVE AND NEGATIVE CHARGES

The basic building blocks of all objects are small particles called **atoms** or **molecules**. Inside an atom or molecule are even smaller particles called protons, neutrons, and electrons.

The **protons** are situated in the centre or nucleus of an atom and are **positively charged**. The **electrons** are **negatively charged** and are continually orbiting the nucleus. The electrostatic force between these opposite charges holds the atom together.

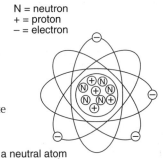

N = neutron
+ = proton
− = electron

a neutral atom

CHARGING BY FRICTION

Normally the number of protons and electrons in an atom is equal. The atom is neutral. But sometimes it is possible for one object to 'steal' electrons from another simply by being rubbed against it.

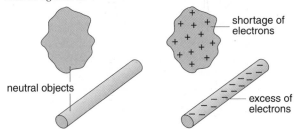

neutral objects

shortage of electrons

excess of electrons

When a polythene rod is rubbed with a cloth some of the cloth's electrons are 'stolen' by the rod. The rod is now negatively charged because it has excess electrons and the cloth is positively charged because it has less electrons. Both objects are said to be charged with **static electricity**.

ATTRACTION AND REPULSION

When two charged objects are brought close together they exert a force on each other.

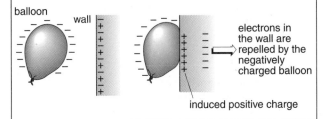

electrostatic repulsion

electrostatic attraction

INDUCED CHARGE

When a balloon is rubbed with a cloth it is possible to 'stick' it on a wall or ceiling. If the balloon is negatively charged by the rubbing it will repel electrons on the surface of the wall. The wall now has an **induced** (positive) **charge** on it. Opposite charges attract so the balloon sticks to the wall.

balloon

wall

electrons in the wall are repelled by the negatively charged balloon

induced positive charge

COMMON EFFECTS/USES OF STATIC ELECTRICITY

- When clothing is worn, it sometimes becomes electrostatically charged ... clinging and crackling as it is taken off.

- Dust is attracted to TV screens and records because they become charged whilst in use.

- Drivers and passengers sometimes receive a small shock when they step out of a car as they have become electrically charged during their journey.

Lightning

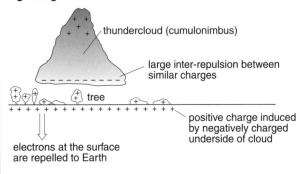

thundercloud (cumulonimbus)

large inter-repulsion between similar charges

tree

positive charge induced by negatively charged underside of cloud

electrons at the surface are repelled to Earth

Thunder clouds contain separated positive and negative charges. If they are present in large enough numbers the inter-repulsion between similar charges is sufficient for the insulation of the air to be broken down and a flash of lightning to occur. The charges escape to Earth where they can avoid the large repulsive forces.

Refuelling aircraft

As an aeroplane travels through the air it becomes charged by friction. If while in this changed state it is refuelled on landing there is a danger that the excess charges will cause a spark as the refuelling nozzle is brought close to the plane, resulting in the highly inflammable petroleum vapours being ignited. To avoid this the plane's tyres are made of special conducting rubber which allows the charge to run to Earth safely.

Electrostatic filters

These are filter used in chimneys to remove dust and ash from gases and fumes which are being released into the atmosphere. The dust is charged as it passes through a mesh near the base of the chimney and is then attracted and sticks to oppositely charged metal plates positioned higher in the chimney.

Electrostatic sprays

These charge the fine droplets of paint as they leave the nozzle. This ensures that the object being sprayed receives an even coat of paint.

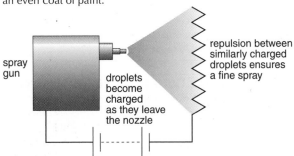

spray gun

droplets become charged as they leave the nozzle

repulsion between similarly charged droplets ensures a fine spray

Photocopiers

Electrostatic photocopiers use special toner powders which stick to the parts of a sheet of paper which have been electrostatically charged.

F2 Currents and circuits

ELECTRIC CURRENT

In a metal such as a piece of wire the atoms are arranged in a regular pattern called a **lattice**. The positive charges within an atom are concentrated in its nucleus and are unable to move. The negative charges ie the electrons are quite a distance away from the positive nucleus and are continually moving. Some of the outermost electrons are able to drift from atom to atom. Under normal circumstances this drift of electrons is haphazard and there is no net flow of charge.

non-metal

no net flow of charge

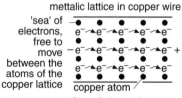

mettalic lattice in copper wire
'sea' of electrons, free to move between the atoms of the copper lattice

copper atom

net flow of charge ie. current

If a cell is connected across the wire more of the electrons will flow towards the positive terminal. This **flow of charge creates an electric current**.

If several cells are connected together the combination is called a battery.

Insulators such as plastics have very few or no loose charges and therefore will not conduct electricity.

ELECTROLYSIS

Some chemical compounds such as lead bromine will not conduct whilst in the form of a solid but will conduct if they are molten or dissolved in water. These **ionic compounds** are made up of electrically charged particles called **ions**, which become mobile when not in the solid state. The current in these *electrolytes* is due to a flow of positive ions to the negative electrode and the negative ions moving to the positive electrode. As a result of this flow of ions simpler substances are released at the electrodes. This process is called **electrolysis**.

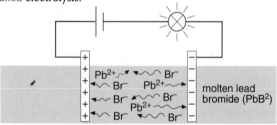

molten lead bromide (PbB^2)

The amount of these simpler substances that form at the electrodes depends upon:

- the size of the current passed through the electrolyte.
- the time the current is passed through the electrolyte
- the chemicals that form the electrolyte

CONVENTIONAL CURRENT/ELECTRON FLOW

When early scientists experimented with electricity they guessed, incorrectly, that it was 'positive'. They assumed that all *electric currents* flowed from positive to negative.

Even though we now know that, in fact, it is a flow of negatively charged electrons from negative to positive, it has been agreed by all scientists to continue to think of electric current as flowing from positive to negative. This is called **conventional current**.

SWITCHES

Current will only flow if a circuit is complete. Switches turn circuits on and off by making them complete or incomplete.

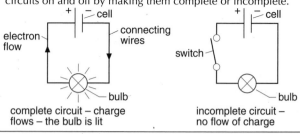

complete circuit – charge flows – the bulb is lit

incomplete circuit – no flow of charge

SERIES AND PARALLEL CIRCUITS

In a **series** circuit the current has only one path to follow. There are no branches. One switch will turn the whole circuit on or off.

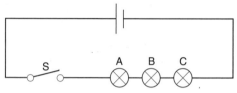

when S is closed bulbs A, B and C light up

In a **parallel** circuit there are several paths the current might follow. Switches can be used to turn the whole or just part of the circuit on and off.

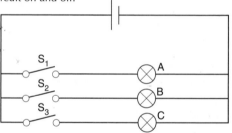

Bulb A will only light up when switch S_1 is closed
Bulb B will only light up when switch S_2 is closed
Bulb C will only light up when switch S_3 is closed

CHARGE AND CURRENT

Electric charge (Q) is measured in **coulombs** (**C**). One coulomb is the equivalent of the charge on approximately six million million million (6×10^{18}) electrons.

Electric current (I) is measured in **amperes** (**A**). *If one coulomb of charge flows past a point in a circuit in one second the current is one ampere.*

Example
If 10 C of charge flow past point P in 2 s the current flowing in the circuit is 5 A.

$$\frac{10\ C}{2\ s} \qquad P \qquad 5\ A$$

If 6 C of charge flow past point P in 3 s the current flowing in the circuit is 2 A.

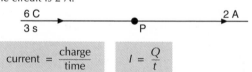

$$\frac{6\ C}{3\ s} \qquad P \qquad 2\ A$$

$$\text{current} = \frac{\text{charge}}{\text{time}} \qquad I = \frac{Q}{t}$$

Where:
I = current in amperes
Q = charge in coulombs
t = time in secs

F3 Circuits and electrical measurements

MEASURING CURRENT

An **ammeter** is used to measure the **current** flowing. It is connected **in series** with the part of the circuit being investigated.

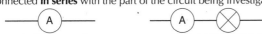

symbol for ammeter   ammeter in series with bulb

In a series circuit the current is the same everywhere.

$$I_1 = I_2 = I_3$$

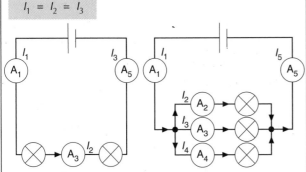

In a **parallel** circuit the currents may differ from place to place but the sum of the currents in the branches of a parallel circuit is equal to the current entering and leaving the network.

$$I_2 + I_3 + I_4 = I_1 = I_5$$

MEASURING VOLTAGE

A **voltmeter** is connected across a component to determine how much electrical energy it is converting. The voltmeter is measuring the **potential difference** or pd across the component.

symbol for voltmeter

Example

If the pd across this bulb is 6 V this means that every time one coulomb of charge passes through the bulb 6 J of electrical energy are converted into 6 J of heat and light energy.

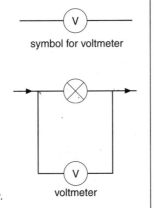

voltmeter

VOLTAGES IN SERIES CIRCUITS

If all the electrical energy the charges receive from the cell is converted into other forms of energy in the external part of the circuit, then the sum of the pds in the external part of the circuit is equal to the pd across the cell.

$$V_c = V_1 + V_2 + V_3$$

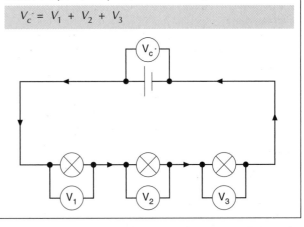

VOLTAGES IN PARALLEL CIRCUITS

In a parallel circuit the pds across all the branches of a network are the same.

$$V_c = V_1 = V_2 = V_3$$

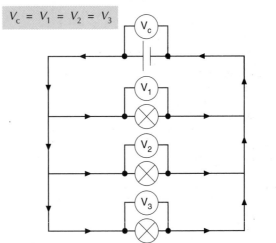

ELECTROMOTIVE FORCE AND POTENTIAL DIFFERENCE

Charges need energy to flow around a circuit. They receive this energy from a power supply such as a cell or battery. The amount of energy given to the charges is determined by the **electromotive force (emf)** of the cell (measured in volts)

One coulomb of charge flowing through a cell of emf 1.5 V will gain 1.5 J of energy.

IN   OUT

charge 1 C   charge 1 C
energy almost nil   energy 1.5 J

The emf of a cell or battery is the amount of energy given to each coulomb of charge that flows through it.

The **potential difference (pd)** (of a component) is the value, measured in volts, between the terminals of a component in a circuit.

As each coloumb of charge travels through the various components in a circuit all the energy it has received from the cell is converted into other forms.

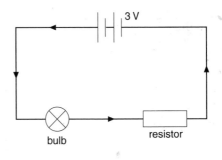

bulb   resistor

In the circuit above each coulomb of charge receives 3 J of energy from the battery. As it then passes through the bulb and resistor nearly all of this electrical energy is converted into heat and light energy. There is almost no energy conversion (energy loss) in the connecting wires.

F4 Resistance

RESISTANCE TO CURRENT FLOW

When current flows through a metallic conductor such as a length of wire electrons move between the atoms of the lattice. If the electrons can do this easily then the piece of wire is said to have a low **resistance**. If it is difficult for the electrons to flow through the wire then we say that it has a high resistance.

The resistance (R) of a piece of wire depends upon:
- the length of the wire.... if the length is doubled the resistance is doubled

- the cross-sectional area of the wire ... if the area is doubled the resistance is halved

- the temperature of the wire ... as the temperature increases the resistance increases (see resistance and temperature)

- the material from which the wire is made (the *resistivity* of the material)

To control the size of the current flowing in a circuit we use **resistors**. These behave like obstacles placed in the path of the current. The resistors have values measured in **ohms** (Ω). A resistor of 100 Ω is a much greater obstacle to the flow of current than a resistor of 10 Ω.

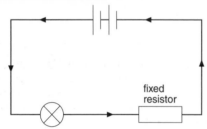

fixed resistor

Variable resistors have values that can be altered so it is possible to adjust the current flowing in the circuit

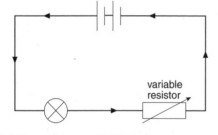

variable resistor

RESISTANCE, TEMPERATURE AND SEMICONDUCTORS

Metallic conductors

At any temperature above zero Kelvin the atoms of a metallic conductor are vibrating. As the temperature is increased the atoms vibrate more violently and it becomes more difficult for the electrons to flow through the lattice structure. *The resistance of a metallic conductor increases with temperature.*

Semiconductors

In semiconducting materials such as silicon and germanium there are far fewer free electrons (charge carriers) than in metallic conductors. The flow of charge through these materials is therefore quite difficult. However if a semiconductor is heated gently more charge carriers become free and the movement of charge through the material is easier ie *the resistance of semiconducting materials decreases as the temperature increases.*

Two of the most common semiconducting components are the **thermistor** and the **light dependent resistor** (**LDR**).

The resistance of a thermistor is very sensitive to changes in temperature. Thermistors are therefore often used in temperature-sensing circuits such as fire alarms or thermostats.

Light dependent resistors are sensitive to changes in light intensity. If a bright light is shone on to an LDR, charge carriers are freed and the resistance of the LDR decreases. LDRs are therefore often used in light-sensitive circuits such as automatic lighting controls or burglar alarms.

thermistor

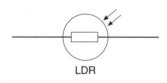

LDR

NETWORKS OF RESISTORS

Very often circuits contain more than one resistor. To work out the overall effect of these networks it is possible to calculate the resultant resistance using a formula.

If the resistors are connected **in series** the total resistance R_T is given by:

$$R_T = r_1 + r_2 + r_3 + r_4 + ...$$

Example

$$R_T = 2\,\Omega + 3\,\Omega + 4\,\Omega + 5\,\Omega$$

$$R_T = 14\,\Omega$$

If several resistors are connected **in parallel** their total resistance R_T can be found using the equation:

$$\frac{1}{R_T} = \frac{1}{r_1} + \frac{1}{r_2} + \frac{1}{r_3}$$

Example

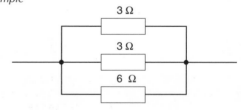

$$\frac{1}{R_T} = \frac{1}{3\,\Omega} + \frac{1}{3\,\Omega} + \frac{1}{6\,\Omega}$$

$$\frac{1}{R_T} = \frac{5}{6}\,\Omega$$

$$R_T = 1.2\,\Omega$$

F5 Ohm's law

CURRENT, VOLTAGE, AND RESISTANCE

It is possible to alter the current flowing in a circuit by:
- altering the resistance in the circuit

- replacing the cell with a battery of larger emf (which would apply a greater voltage or pd across the wire).

In 1826 a scientist called George Ohm carried out a series of experiments to try to discover the relationship between the current flowing through a conductor (resistor) and the potential difference applied across its ends.

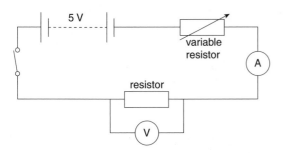

When the switch was closed the current flowing through the resistor was noted from the ammeter and the pd across the wire was noted from the voltmeter. The value of the variable resistor was then altered and a new pair of readings noted. This was repeated several times and the results put into a table.

Typical results

p.d/volts	I/amps
0.0	0.0
1.0	0.2
2.0	0.4
3.0	0.8
4.0	1.0
5.0	1.2

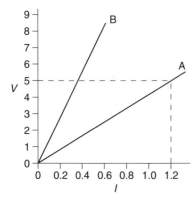

Ohm's results produced a straight line graph passing through the origin. From this he concluded that:

> *the current flowing through a resistor is directly proportional to the potential difference across its ends providing the temperature remains constant.* This is **Ohm's Law**.

$$resistance = \frac{voltage}{current}$$

$$R = \frac{V}{I}$$

$$V = I \times R$$

Ohm repeated his experiments several times with different conductors. He still obtained a straight line graph but the gradients were different. The graph for a good conductor (A) would have a small gradient, whilst the graph for a poor conductor (B) would be quite steep.

The gradient of the graph is the **resistance** of the conductor.

The resistance of A on the graph $= 4.16\ \Omega$

Example
If a current of 2 A flows through a piece of wire of resistance 6 Ω, calculate the pd across the ends of the wire.

$$V = I \times R$$
$$V = 2 \times 6$$
$$V = 12\ V$$

Example
If a current of 1.5 A flows through a piece of wire when a pd of 10 V is applied across its ends calculate the resistance of the wire.

$$R = \frac{V}{I}$$
$$R = \frac{10\ V}{1.5}$$
$$R = 6.6\ \Omega$$

OHMIC AND NON-OHMIC CONDUCTORS

A component or material which produces a straight line graph through the origin and obeys Ohm's Law is called an **ohmic conductor**. Some components do not obey Ohm's Law. they are non-ohmic components.

As the current flowing through a filament bulb increases the the resistance increases, so the gradient of the graph becomes steeper. It is a non-ohmic conductor.

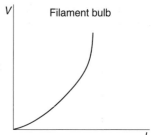

A diode is a resistor which only allows current to flow through it in one direction. It therefore acts like a non-ohmic conductor.

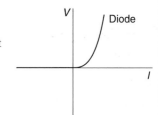

Gases are also non-ohmic conductors.

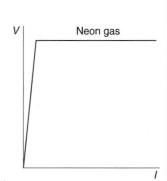

F6 Electricity in the home (1)

LIVE, NEUTRAL, AND EARTH

Most homes are connected to the National Grid by a supply cable. Upon entering the home the supply enters a consumer box where it is divided into several different circuits: upstairs; downstairs; lighting. Circuits contain three wires: Live; Neutral; Earth (safety wire).

The electricity 'enters' the circuits by the live wire and 'returns' by the Neutral wire. The earth wire is included in a circuit to protect the user from receiving an electric shock should something in the circuit be faulty.

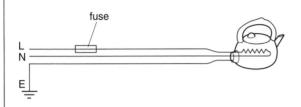

The kettle in this circuit is in good working order. When it is turned on electrical energy will flow into it through the live wire and the circuit is completed by the neutral.

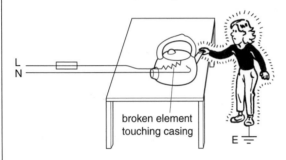

This kettle is not in good working order. The broken heating filament cannot be seen by the user. When this kettle is turned on the user becomes part of the circuit, in place of the neutral wire. Under these circumstances the user will receive a serious, possibly fatal, electric shock.

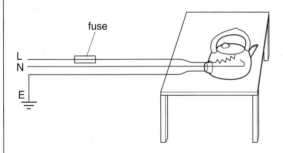

This kettle is also not in good working order. But when turned on the earth wire, which is connected to the outer casing, provides a route for the electrical energy to flow through rather than through the body of the user. Under these circumstances the fuse will blow turning off the supply to the kettle.

Double insulation

In circuits where there is no earth wire (and even in some circuits where there is an earth wire) the user can be protected from faulty appliances by **double insulation**. The appliance is enclosed in a plastic, non-conducting outer case so that there is no possibility of electrical energy passing through them.

PLUGS

Connection to the mains supply is made for all appliances through a plug. Plugs are designed to ensure that the user of an appliance is kept safe.

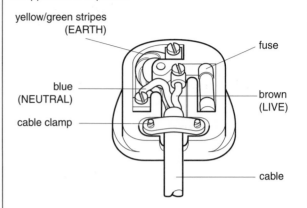

For the plug to provide safe connection to the mains it is essential that the pins are wired correctly, there are no loose or cut wires and the correct fuse is fitted.

SWITCHES

One reason why it is extremely important to connect the correct wire to the correct pin in a plug is because of the effect this has on the positioning of switches.

If a switch is connected to the live wire it isolates the appliance ie no electrical energy can reach it. The user is safe from electric shock.

If a plug is wired incorrectly so that the switch is now connected to the neutral wire the appliance is not isolated. Electrical energy can still flow into it and the user become part of the return circuit.

FUSES

If an appliance becomes faulty there is a danger that too much current may flow in a circuit which could damage the appliance or harm the user. To avoid this problem fuses are included in most household circuits and to appliances.

If too much current passes through the thin fuse wire it becomes too hot and melts. The circuit is now incomplete and current stops flowing. By using wires of different thicknesses and metals it is possible to choose a fuse which will allow a circuit to work properly but which will turn the circuit off if the current exceeds a certain value. The most common fuses are rated at 1 A, 3 A, and 13 A. The most appropriate fuse for an appliance requiring a current of 2.5 A to work properly would be the 3 A fuse. The most appropriate fuse for an appliance requiring a current of 5 A to work properly would be the 13 A fuse.

Some appliances experience a surge of current when they are switched on. They may require a higher rated fuse.

F7 Electricity in the home (2)

CIRCUITS BREAKERS

Some modern fuses are in the form of a *trip switch*. If the current exceeds a certain value an electromagnet separates a pair of contacts and turns the circuit off. These circuit breakers work far faster than the normal fuse and so offer greater protection. Also the circuit breakers can be reset at the press of a button rather than having to be replaced.

Mains electricity can be lethal, for example if a gardener cuts through the mains cable to his hedge cutters or lawn mower there is a real danger of them receiving an electric shock. **Residual current circuit breakers** are designed to prevent this. They compare the currents in the live and neutral wires and break the circuit very rapidly if there is any difference.

ELECTRICAL POWER

Light bulbs often have two numbers printed on them.

 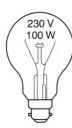

230 V
60 W

230 V
100 W

The first number is the voltage rating: 230 V.
This indicates that for each coulomb of charge that passes through the bulb 230 joules of electrical energy are converted into 230 joules of heat and light energy.
The second number is the power rating: ... W. This tells us how rapidly this conversion is taking place. In a 60 W bulb 60 joules of electrical energy are being converted into 60 joules of heat and light energy every second. The second bulb is brighter because it is converting 100 joules of energy per second. The power rating of these two bulbs is 60 W and 100 W respectively.

Typical power ratings for household appliances:

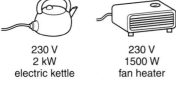

230 V	230 V	230 V
2 kW	1500 W	1 kW
electric kettle	fan heater	one bar electric fire

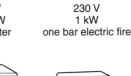

230 V	230 V	230 V
500 W	1 kW	650 W
electric iron	washing machine	colour television

230 V	230 V
1250 W	60 W
hair dryer	lamp

The power of an appliance is related to the voltage across it and the current flowing through it by the equation

> power = voltage × current
>
> $P = V \times I$

Example
When a three bar electric fire is turned on a current of 12.5 A flows through it. If the pd across the fire is 230 V calculate the power of the fire

$P = V \times I$

$P = 230\text{ V} \times 12.5\text{ A}$

$P = 2875\text{ W}$ or approximately 3 kW

To calculate the total energy converted

$E = P \times t$ where t is the time in seconds

$E = V \times I \times t$

How much energy is converted by the above fire in 5 mins?

$E = P \times t$

$E = 2875 \times 5 \times 60$

$E = 862500\text{ J}$ or approximately 900 kJ

Paying for domestic electricity

From the above example you can see that the number of joules of electrical energy used by a normal household every three months will be enormous. It will be far too clumsy a number to be of any use. To get round this problem electricity boards measure electrical energy supplies in much bigger quantities called **units**.

A 1 kW fire which is turned on for 1 hour will use one unit of energy. Similarly a 2 kW fire turned on for 4 hours will use 8 units of energy.

> number of units used = kilowatts × time in hours

One unit is also known as one **kilowatt hour**.

Example
What is the cost of leaving a 3 kW fire turned on for 4 hours if one unit of energy costs 12p

units used = 3 kW × 4 hrs

units used = 12

cost = units used × cost of one unit

cost = 12 units × 12p

= £1.44

F8 Basic magnetism

MAGNETS

A magnet has the ability to attract certain materials such as iron, steel, nickel, and cobalt. These are called **magnetic materials**. Materials which it cannot attract such as copper, tin, wood, and plastic are called **non-magnetic materials**.

The strongest parts of a magnet are called its **poles**. Most magnets have two poles .... a **north-seeking** and a **south-seeking** pole.

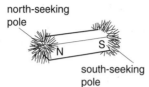

north-seeking pole

south-seeking pole

If a bar magnet is suspended so that it is free to rotate horizontally it will gradually come to rest with its north-seeking pole pointing northwards and its south-seeking pole pointing southwards. It is behaving as a **simple compass**.

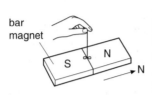

bar magnet

N

north-seeking pole

paper stirrup

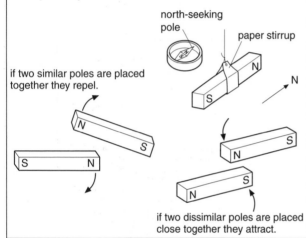

if two similar poles are placed together they repel.

if two dissimilar poles are placed close together they attract.

DOMAIN THEORY OF MAGNETISM

The domain theory of magnetism suggests that a magnetic materials such as iron contains within its structure tiny cells called **domains** and that mini molecular magnets exist inside these domains.

In an **unmagnetised** piece of iron all the mini magnets within a particular domain point in the same direction but in each neighbouring domain they point in different directions. The result of this is that the magnetic effect of the domains cancel each other out.

In a **magnetised** piece of iron all the domains are lined up so that their magnetic effects reinforce each other.

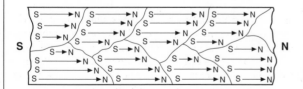

MAGNETICALLY HARD AND MAGNETICALLY SOFT MATERIALS.

The domains in some materials are very easy to put into and out of line. These materials are said to be magnetically soft and are fairly easy to magnetise and demagnetise. Iron is a magnetically soft material.

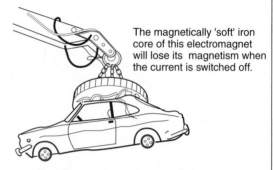

The magnetically 'soft' iron core of this electromagnet will lose its magnetism when the current is switched off.

Some materials such as steel are magnetically hard. The domains are quite difficult to line up but having done so they will remain in place. This is why steel is an excellent material for permanent magnets but of no use in electromagnets.

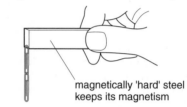

magnetically 'hard' steel keeps its magnetism

MAGNETIC FIELDS.

Around a magnetised object such as a bar magnet, there is a volume of space where the effects of magnetism can be detected. This space is called a **magnetic field**. Its shape and direction can be discovered using iron filings or plotting compasses.

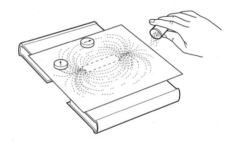

Magnetic lines of force:

- show the shape of the magnetic field
- show the strength of the magnetic field ... the field is strongest where the magnetic lines of force are close together
- always travel from the north-seeking pole to the south-seeking pole.

INTERACTING MAGNETIC FIELDS

If two bar magnets are placed close together their magnetic fields will interact and produce a new pattern of magnetic lines of force. From these patterns, it is possible to say if the magnetic forces are forces of attraction or forces of repulsion.

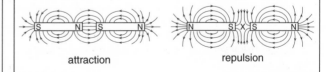

attraction

repulsion

F9 Electromagnetism

ELECTROMAGNETIC FIELDS

When an electric current is passed through a piece of wire a magnetic field is created around it. The field is cylindrical in shape and strongest close to the wire.

If the direction of the current is reversed so too is the direction of the magnetic field.

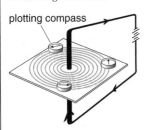
plotting compass

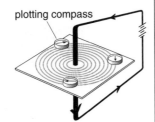
plotting compass

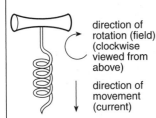

direction of rotation (field) (clockwise viewed from above)

direction of movement (current)

The direction of the magnetic field can be predicted by imagining a cork screw being turned so that it moves in the same direction as the current. The rotation of the screw indicates the direction of the magnetic field.

Coils and solenoids

The field created by current flowing through a single piece of wire is quite weak but by wrapping the wire into a coil or solenoid a much stronger field can be produced.

The shape of the field produced by a coil is similar to that produced by a bar magnet.

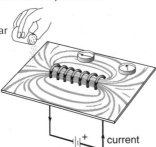

current

The polarity of the magnetic field can be determined by looking at one end of the coil and deciding if the current is flowing clockwise or anticlockwise

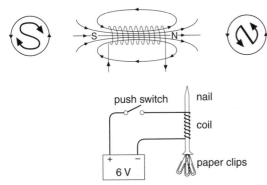

push switch   nail
coil
paper clips
6 V

The main factors which determine the strength of the magnetic field produced by a coil or solenoid are:

- the size of the current flowing through the coil
- the number of turns on the coil
- the cross-sectional area of the coil
- what the coil is wrapped around. (Wrapping it around a magnetisable material such as soft iron creates a stronger magnetic field.)

USING ELECTROMAGNETS

The two main advantages an electromagnet has compared to a permanent magnet are:

- it can be turned on and off

- its magnetic field can be adjusted to make it stronger or weaker or change its polarity

In a scrapyard it wouldn't be possible to pick up and drop old cars using a permanent magnet, but it can be done using an electromagnet.

Electric Bell

When the button is pressed the circuit is complete and current flows. The soft iron core becomes magnetised and attracts the iron armature. As the hammer strikes the bell the armature pulls away from the contract screw and the circuit is no longer complete. Current ceases to flow, the soft iron core is no longer magnetised and so the armature is pulled back to its original position.

The circuit is once more complete and the cycle begins again. As long as the button is pressed the bell will ring.

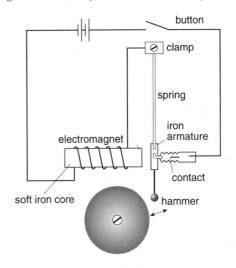

button
clamp
spring
iron armature
electromagnet
contact
soft iron core
hammer

Relay Switches

A relay is a switch which uses the magnetic effect of a current flowing in one circuit to control the current flowing in a another. This may be particularly useful if the current flowing in the second circuit is very large and possibly dangerous.

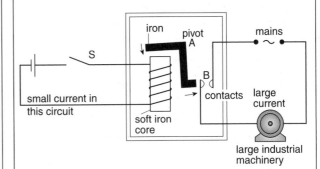

iron   pivot A   mains
S
small current in this circuit
B   contacts   large current
soft iron core
large industrial machinery

When the switch S is closed the circuit is complete and current flows in the switching circuit. The soft iron core becomes magnetised and attracts the soft iron armature. The armature pivots around point A and in so doing pushes the contacts at B together. This second circuit is now complete and turned on. If the switch S is opened the field collapses, the armature returns to its original position, the contacts will open and the secondary circuit is turned off.

F10 Electromagnetic forces

THE MOTOR PRINCIPLE

If a wire carrying a current is placed between the poles of a magnet the wire experiences a force due to the overlap and interaction between the two magnetic fields.

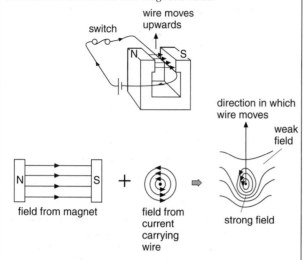

field from magnet + field from current carrying wire ⇒ strong field / weak field / direction in which wire moves

The size of the force can be increased by increasing the strength of the magnetic field or increasing the size of the current in the wire.

The direction of the force experienced by the wire depends both on the direction of the current in the wire and the direction of the of the magnet's magnetic field.

FLEMING'S LEFT HAND RULE

Using Fleming's left hand rule the direction of the force/motion can be predicted.

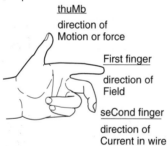

thuMb
direction of Motion or force

First finger
direction of Field

seCond finger
direction of Current in wire

MOVING COIL LOUDSPEAKER

The signals sent from the amplifier of a stereo system to its speakers are in the form of small electric currents which are continually changing in size and direction. As they pass through the coil situated between the poles of a permanent magnet it is made to move very rapidly back and forth. This in turn causes the cone to vibrate, so producing the sound waves we hear.

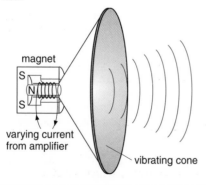

magnet

varying current from amplifier

vibrating cone

THE SIMPLE DC MOTOR

If two pieces of wire are placed between the poles of a magnet and current passed through them in opposite directions one wire will feel a force pushing it upwards whilst the second will feel a force pushing it downwards. If the two pieces of wire are opposite sides of a coil, the coil will begin to rotate. This is the basic principle of the electric motor.

⊙ is the symbol for current flowing out of the paper
⊗ is the symbol for current flowing into the paper

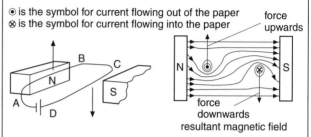

force upwards / force downwards / resultant magnetic field

After turning through 90° the coil ABCD will come to a halt. If the rotation is to continue AB which was going up must now move down and CD which was going down must now move up. To obtain this change in direction a split ring or commutator is used. This has the effect of changing the direction of the current in the coil after every half turn.

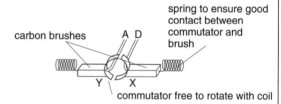

carbon brushes

spring to ensure good contact between commutator and brush

commutator free to rotate with coil

If at the start X is connected to the positive terminal of the cell current will flow around the coil in the direction DCBA and the coil will rotate clockwise.

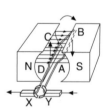

As the coil passes the vertical X becomes connected to the negative terminal of the cell, the current now flows in the opposite direction ABCD and the coil continues to rotate clockwise.

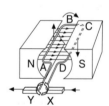

In real motors it is important that the turning motion is smooth. To achieve this the single coil is replaced by several interlocked coils and the permanent magnets are replaced by curved electromagnets.

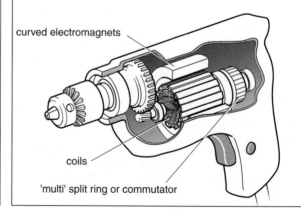

curved electromagnets

coils

'multi' split ring or commutator

F11 Generators and dynamos

ELECTROMAGNETIC INDUCTION

If a conductor such as a piece of wire is moved through a magnetic field cutting magnetic lines of force a voltage or emf will be induced across its ends. The process which produces the emf is called **electromagnetic induction**. If the wire is part of a complete circuit the induced emf will cause a current to flow.

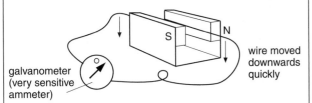

galvanometer
(very sensitive ammeter)

wire moved downwards quickly

The size and direction of the induced emf depends upon:

• The speed at which the magnetic lines of force are cut.

• The number of wires/coils cutting the magnetic lines of force

• The strength of the magnetic field.

The direction of the induced emf depends upon:

• The direction of the motion

• The direction of the magnetic field

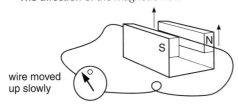

wire moved up slowly

You can predict the direction of the induced emf using **Fleming's right hand rule**.

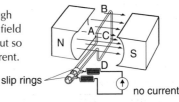

ThuMb   Movement of conductor
First finger   direction of magnetic field
SeCond finger Direction of induced Current

ThuMb
First finger
SeCond finger
RIGHT hand

Current can also be generated by moving a bar magnet in or out of a coil.

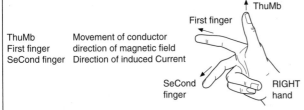

magnet moving forward

galvanometer

magnet moving back

galvanometer

LENZ'S LAW

The direction of the current induced in a coil can be found using Lenz's law. This states that *the direction of the induced emf/current is such as to oppose the change that is creating it.*

If the north-seeking pole of a magnet is pushed into a coil, current will be induced which will create a magnetic field around the coil. This field will oppose the movement of the magnet and a north pole will be created at the top of the coil. The current will flow anticlockwise. Pulling the magnet out will cause the induced current to flow clockwise, producing a south pole which tries to prevent the magnet from being pulled out.

SIMPLE DYNAMO

As the wheel of the bicycle turns the magnet inside the dynamo is made to rotate. As it does so its magnetic field cuts through the wires of the coil. The induced current which this creates can be used to work the bicycle's lights.

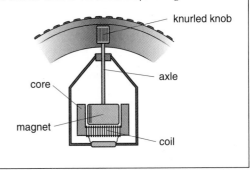

knurled knob

axle

core

magnet

coil

SIMPLE AC GENERATOR

When a coil is rotated between the poles of a magnet its wires cut through magnetic field lines (flux) causing a current to flow. The size and direction of the induced current changes as the coil rotates. This is the basic principle behind the simple ac generator.

As the coil moves through the vertical position no field lines of flux are being cut so there is no induced current.

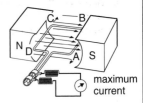

slip rings

no current

As the coil moves through the horizontal position lines of flux are being cut by AB and CD at the maximum rate. A large current is induced.

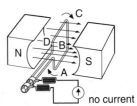

maximum current

As the coil passes the vertical position for a second time there is again no induced current.

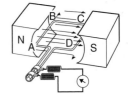

no current

As the coil passes through the horizontal position for a second time a large current is again induced but flowing in the opposite direction.

maximum current but in the opposite direction to position (b)

A current which flows back and forth like this is called an alternating or ac current.

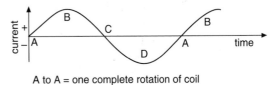

A to A = one complete rotation of coil

F12 Transformers

INDUCTION BETWEEN TWO COILS

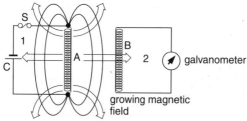

growing magnetic field

When switch S is closed, current will begin to flow around circuit 1. As its value increases from zero a magnetic field will grow outwards from coil A. As it does so some of its magnetic lines of force will cut through the wires of coil B causing a current to flow in circuit 2.

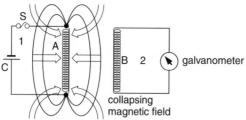

collapsing magnetic field

If switch S is now opened current will cease to flow in circuit 1. The field around coil A will collapse and as it does so, a current will again be induced in circuit 2 but in the opposite direction.

A soft iron core placed through the centres of both coils produces an increase in the size of the induced current. This is because the core increases the magnetic field strength around the two coils causing the magnetic lines of force to cut through the coil B at a greater rate. This combination of two coils linked together by a soft iron core is called a transformer.

In the above example a current is only induced in circuit 2 whilst the magnetic field of coil A is growing and collapsing. If the cell C is replaced by an ac supply the magnetic field around coil A will change continually and a current will therefore be continually being induced in circuit 2.

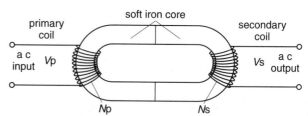

The size of the induced voltage in circuit 2 depends upon the number of turns on each coil and the size of of the applied voltage in circuit 1. The relationship between these four values is shown below.

$$\frac{\text{number of turns on the primary coil}}{\text{number of turns on the secondary}} = \frac{\text{applied voltage}}{\text{Induced voltage}}$$

$$\frac{N_p}{N_s} = \frac{V_p}{V_s}$$

This equation is true if the transformer is 100% efficient. In practice some energy is lost mainly in the form of heat. To keep these losses to a minimum:

- thick copper wire is used for both coils to reduce the heating effect of the current

- both coils are linked with a soft iron core to concentrate the magnetic field around the coils

- the soft iron core is laminated to reduce eddy currents being generated in the core by the moving magnetic field.

The main purpose of a transformer is to alter voltages. If a transformer is used to *increase* voltage (and thereby reduce current) it is called a **step-up transformer**. If a transformer is used to *decrease* voltage (and thereby increase current), it is called a **step-down transformer**. Both step-up and step-down transformers are used in the National Grid.

TRANSMISSION OF ELECTRICITY VIA THE NATIONAL GRID

At power stations, coal, oil, gas, or nuclear material provide the energy necessary to drive steam turbines which then turn ac generators to produce the electrical energy we require. This electrical energy is then transmitted along the National Grid into our homes. As it passes along the cables and wire much of the energy could be wasted by the current causing the wires to become warm. To prevent this the output from the generators is fed into a large step-up transformer which decreases the size of the current and increases the size of the voltage.

Well away from towns and cities this dangerous high voltage supply is supported high in the air by pylons.

Close to towns where the energy is required the voltage is reduced (and the current increased) in stages by step-down transformers.

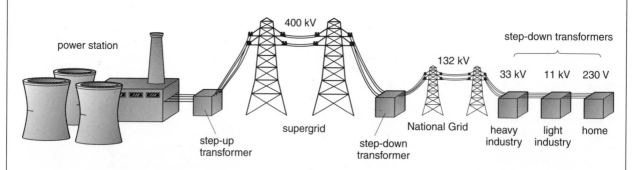

Although it is possible to manipulate dc currents and voltages using resistors, it is much easier and far more efficient to use ac supplies and to use extremely efficient transformers.

F13 Electronic systems and control

THE SYSTEMS APPROACH

To use a stereo system or a TV set it is not necessary to understand the workings of the electrical circuits it contains. It is sufficient to know that by carrying out a particular action, pressing a button or turning a knob, the required result is obtained. The sound becomes louder, or the picture becomes brighter This *black box* treatment of circuits is called the **systems** approach.

The information, which the processor in the centre of these systems is handling, must be in the form of an electric current or voltage. In order to change information into this form input devices such as microphones, thermistors, or LDRs are used. Devices such as these are called **transducers**. When the information has been processed it needs to be changed back into a form that we human beings can handle. To do this, output transducers such as loudspeakers, light bulbs, LEDs, or buzzers, can be used.

There can be clear advantages to the systems approach.

Most electronic systems can be represented by simple (box) block diagrams.

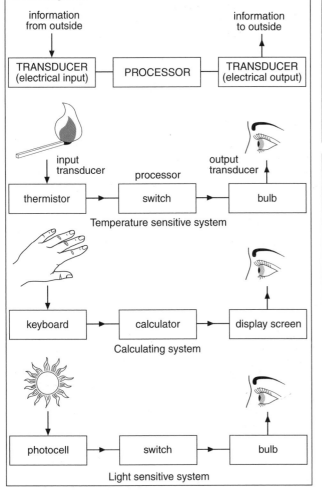

Temperature sensitive system

Calculating system

Light sensitive system

ANALOG AND DIGITAL SYSTEMS

Some electronic systems have processors which manipulate input signals in a continuous manner. These are called analog systems.

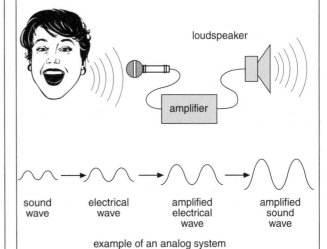

| sound wave | electrical wave | amplified electrical wave | amplified sound wave |

example of an analog system

The waves before and after amplification are continuous. This is an analog amplification system.

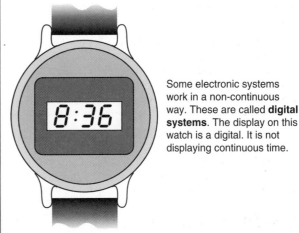

Some electronic systems work in a non-continuous way. These are called **digital systems**. The display on this watch is a digital. It is not displaying continuous time.

BINARY CODE

Digital processors such as computers handle information and perform calculations using a number system called binary. Instead of using ten different digits the processors use just two: 1 and 0. These numbers can be represented by switches which have two possible states or conditions: ON or OFF.

Number	Binary code
0	0000
1	0001
2	0010
3	0011
4	0100
5	0101
6	0110
7	0111
8	1000
9	1001

F14 Logic

LOGIC GATES

The processors of most electronic systems contain an arrangement of **switches called logic gates**. These switches process the input signals by only allowing them to pass through if they fulfil certain conditions.

There are several different types of gates. *Truth tables* are used to explain 'in a simple away' the results of all the possible combinations of inputs.

The table below summarises the properties of the most common types of gate.

Example of use of gates
Burglar alarm
Connecting several gates together can produce quite sophisticated systems. There are several different methods by which a burglar can be detected using this system.

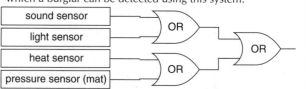

GATE TYPE	SYMBOL	TRUTH TABLE			GATE OPERATION

AND

Input X	Input Y	Output
0	0	0
1	0	0
0	1	0
1	1	1

There is only an output from the AND gate when there is an input to X AND to Y.

This gate might use the conditions of the two sets of doors of an electric lift to control the motor. Unless both doors are closed the lift will not work.

OR

Input X	Input Y	Output
0	0	0
1	0	1
0	1	1
1	1	1

There is an output from the OR gate if there is an input to X OR an input to Y.

This kind of gate could be used to control the barriers, bells, and lights at a railway crossing. If there is a train approaching from one direction OR the opposite direction OR both directions there would be an output.

NOT

Input X	Output
0	1
1	0

There is an output from the NOT gate if there is NOT an input to X.

There is NO output from the NOT gate if there IS an input into X.

This kind of gate is often called an *inverter* gate The processor for automatic street lights almost certainly will contain a NOT gate.

NAND

Input X	Input Y	Output
0	0	1
0	1	1
1	0	1
1	1	0

There is NO output from the NAND gate if there is an input at X AND at Y.

This kind of gate could be used to turn on a warning light or buzzer if either the driver of a car or his passenger are not wearing their seat belts.

NOR

Input X	Input Y	Output
0	0	1
0	1	0
1	0	0
1	1	0

There is NO output from the NOR gate if there is an input at X OR Y.

G1 Kinetic theory (1)

KINETIC THEORY OF SOLIDS

All solids are made up of tiny particles: atoms or molecules. These are often arranged in a regular pattern called a **lattice**. Within a lattice there are electrostatic forces which hold the particles (molecules) in place but allow them to vibrate from side to side. It is these strong intermolecular forces which are responsible for the firmness and rigidity of solids.

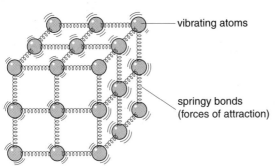

a model of a solid at a temperature above absolute zero

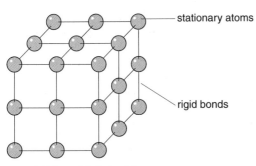

a model of a solid at absolute zero

When a solid is cooled the internal energy of the lattice decreases. The molecular vibrations lessen. Eventually if a solid is cooled to 0 K or –273 °C the vibrations stop. The solid has no internal energy.

Evidence to support the kinetic theory of solids

- Some solids such as common salt or copper sulphate form crystals which are always the **same shape**.

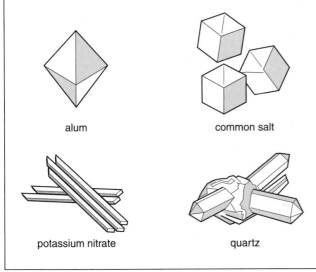

alum

common salt

potassium nitrate

quartz

- It is possible using a sharp blade to cleave crystals. The blade passes between the planes of atoms or molecules.

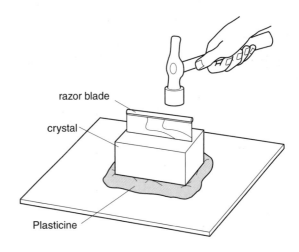

razor blade

crystal

Plasticine

Melting
When a solid is heated the internal energy of the lattice increases and the molecular vibrations become more violent. Eventually if enough energy is given to the solid the vibrations become so violent that the lattice structure begins to break down. There is now no large rigid structure but rather large groups of molecules which are able to flow past each other. The solid has melted.

The energy which is needed to break down the lattice structure in order to produce a liquid is called the **latent heat of fusion**. The temperature remains unchanged whilst the solid melts. All the energy being provided is being used to break down the lattice structure.

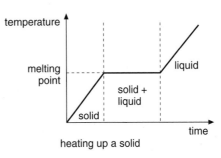

heating up a solid

If a liquid is solidifying the lattice structure is reforming and energy is being released. During this time the temperature of the liquid/solid mixture remains constant.

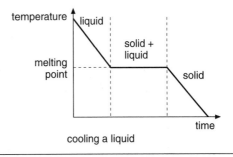

cooling a liquid

G2 Kinetic theory (2)

KINETIC THEORY OF LIQUIDS

Liquids have no particular shape. They will take the shape of the container they are placed in. There is therefore, on the microscopic level, no regular structure. Instead the atoms and molecules exist as large groups. Each group is held together by intermolecular forces but they able to move and slide past neighbouring groups. A liquid has the ability to **flow**.

Evidence to support the kinetic theory of liquids

If a small amount of dye, in the form of a crystal, is added to a beaker of water, its colour gradually spreads throughout the liquid. This suggests that the molecules are sufficiently free to be able to move around. This mixing caused by molecular motion is called **diffusion**. If the water molecules were in a rigid structure and therefore unable to move the colour from the dye would remain in the same place.

clear water
coloured water
potassium permanganate crystal
dissolving crystal

diffusion in water

EVAPORATING

In a liquid individual molecules and groups of molecules have different energies. Some are vibrating and moving around faster than others. If they gain sufficient energy it is possible for the more energetic molecules to escape the attractive intermolecular forces of the liquid and become a gas. This process of individual molecules escaping is called **evaporation**.

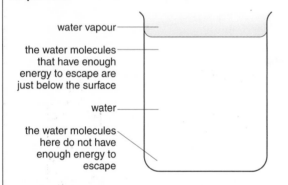

water vapour

the water molecules that have enough energy to escape are just below the surface

water

the water molecules here do not have enough energy to escape

The temperature of a liquid determines the average energy its molecules have. If some of the higher energy molecules escape the average energy of those left behind will decrease and the temperature of the liquid will fall. Evaporation causes cooling of the remaining liquid. Animals use this idea as a means of keeping cool. When hot they sweat. This then evaporates, taking energy from the bodies of the animals and cooling them down.

Factors affecting the rate of evaporation

The rate at which a liquid evaporates depends upon

- temperature ... the hotter the liquid the larger the number of molecules that have enough energy to escape

- surface area ... the larger the surface area the greater the number of molecules just under the surface with the possibility to escape

- movement of air over the surface ... some molecules having escaped through the surface of a liquid almost immediately fall back in.
  (If they are removed before they can fall back the rate of evaporation will increase.)

- Air pressure ... some molecules, having escaped, collide with air molecules immediately above the liquid surface and so fall back in.

  (If the number of air molecules above the surface is reduced evaporation will take place more quickly.)

THE REFRIGERATOR

As the liquid (freon) passes through the freezer unit it evaporates. The energy needed to do this is taken from the interior of the fridge and its contents ie they are kept cool. At the rear of the fridge the vapour is forced by a pump to return to the liquid state before the whole process begins again.

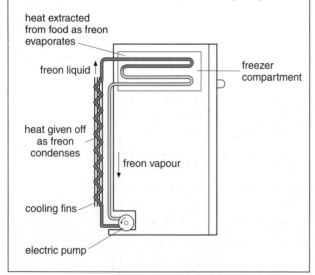

heat extracted from food as freon evaporates

freon liquid

freezer compartment

heat given off as freon condenses

freon vapour

cooling fins

electric pump

BOILING

If the temperature of a liquid is gradually increased, more and more of its molecules gain sufficient energy to escape. Eventually a temperature is reached where the average kinetic energy of the molecules is high enough for them all to escape ie all the groups of molecules break up because of the violence of the molecular vibrations. At this stage the liquid is changing to a gas. It is boiling. Boiling takes place at a fixed temperature.

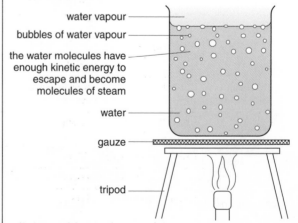

water vapour

bubbles of water vapour

the water molecules have enough kinetic energy to escape and become molecules of steam

water

gauze

tripod

G3 Kinetic theory (3)

COMPARISON OF BOILING AND EVAPORATION

Evaporation

1) Takes place over a range of temperatures

2) Takes place at the surface of the liquid

3) Is affected by pressure

4) Is affected by surface area and wind

Boiling

1) Takes place at one temperature

2) Takes place throughout the liquid

3) Is also affected by pressure

4) Is not affected by surface area and wind

KINETIC THEORY OF GASES

In a gas the atoms and molecules are almost completely free ie they experience no intermolecular forces. For this reason they will fill any container into which they are introduced. The molecules are moving around at high speeds (approximately 500 m/s) even at room temperature, and in all directions.

Evidence to support the kinetic theory of gases
Brownian motion
If some smoke particles are introduced into a smoke cell they can be seen through a microscope moving around in a totally random manner (**Brownian motion**). This happens because they are being continually jostled by extremely small but very fast-moving molecules of air. A similar motion can be seen in liquids using grains of pollen rather than smoke particles.

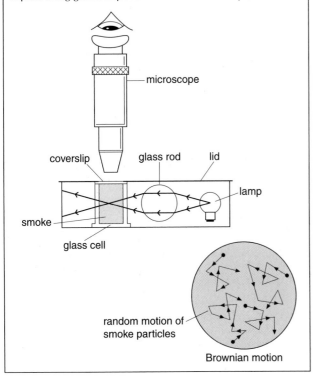

Brownian motion

DIFFUSION IN GASES

If a small amount of scent or perfume is released into a room within a few minutes its odour can be detected in all parts. This is because the molecular motions of the air have caused the aroma to spread or **diffuse**.

This diffusion can be seen if one of the gases is coloured.

Example
Brown nitrogen dioxide is in fact more dense than air and therefore one might expect it to remain at the bottom of the two gas jars. But after a few minutes the brown gas can be seen throughout. The two gases have diffused through each other.

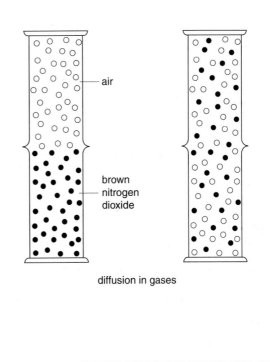

diffusion in gases

SUMMARY

	Solid	Liquid	Gas
Structure	Regular, rigid lattice	No fixed structure	No fixed structure
Intermolecular forces	Strong	Quite strong	None
Molecular spacing	Small	Small	Very large
Degree of freedom	Low	Higher than a solid	Completely free
Kinetic energy	Low	Higher than a solid	Higher than a liquid or a solid

G4 Specific and latent heats

SPECIFIC HEAT CAPACITY (C)

When an object is heated, the energy it receives usually causes an increase in temperature. The size of the temperature increases depends upon:

- how much energy is given to the object (H)

- how much there is of the object ie its mass (m).

- the material from which the object is made (specific heat capacity (C)).

If equal masses of water and oil are given the same amount of energy, the oil would increase in temperature by nearly twice as much as the water. This is because the water has a bigger appetite for energy. It has a bigger specific heat capacity (C).

> The **specific heat capacity** of a substance (C) is the energy necessary to raise the temperature of 1 kg of that substance by 1 °C (or 1 K).

Water has a specific heat capacity of 4200 J/kg/K ie 4200 J of energy would be needed to increase the temperature of 1 kg of water by 1 K.

Substance	Specific heat capacity (J/kg K)
water	4200
ice	2100
copper	380
lead	140

Formula

$$H = m \times C(T_2 - T_1)$$

Example
How much energy is needed to raise the temperature of a 3 kg block of iron from 15 °C to 65 °C? The specific heat capacity of iron is 460 J/kg/K.

Using:
$$H = m \times C\ (T_2 - T_1)$$
$$= 3\ \text{kg} \times 460\ \text{J/kg K} \times 50\ °C$$
$$= 69000\ \text{J or } 69\ \text{kJ}$$

To determine the specific heat capacity of a solid/liquid
The solid/liquid is weighed to find its mass (m). Its temperature is measured (T_1). The electric heater is turned on and the stop clock is started. When the temperature has risen 10 °C (T_2) the stopclock is stopped and the time is noted for which the solid/liquid has been heated (t). The heater is turned off.

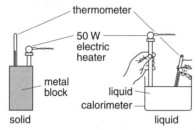

- thermometer
- 50 W electric heater
- metal block
- liquid
- calorimeter
- solid
- liquid

Energy provided by the heater = energy absorbed by the solid/liquid.

$$P \times t = m \times C \times (T_2 - T_1)$$

$$C = \frac{P \times t}{m \times (T_2 - T_1)}$$

In this case:
$$C = \frac{50\ \text{W} \times t}{m \times 10\ °C}$$

TYPICAL HEATING (COOLING) CURVE

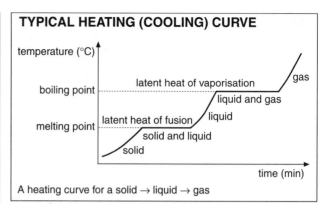

A heating curve for a solid → liquid → gas

SPECIFIC LATENT HEAT

The **specific latent heat of fusion** of a substance is numerically equal to the energy required to change 1 kg of the substance from solid to liquid without temperature change.

To determine the specific latent heat of fusion of ice
The heater is turned on. When the ice is melting freely, the water which drops from the funnel is collected over a period of time (t), eg 200 s. The water collected is weighed to find its mass (m).

If the energy provided by the heater equals the energy taken in by the ice in melting

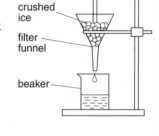

- 50 W electric heater
- crushed ice
- filter funnel
- beaker

$$P \times t = m \times L$$

$$L = \frac{P \times t}{m}$$

In this case:
$$L = \frac{50 \times 200\ \text{s}}{m}$$

The accepted value of the specific latent heat of fusion of ice is 336000 J/kg

> The **specific latent heat of vaporization** of a substance is numerically equal to the quantity of energy required to change 1 kg of the substance from liquid to vapour without temperature change.

To determine the specific latent heat of vaporization of water
A 3 kW electric kettle is suspended from a balance. The kettle is turned on. When the water is boiling freely, the mass of the kettle and water (m_1) is noted down and the stopclock is started. After 300 s the mass of the kettle and water (m_2) is again noted. The kettle is turned off. The mass of the water which has been boiled away is noted ($m_1 - m_2$).

If the energy provided by the heater equals the energy taken in by the water when boiling

$$P \times t = (m_1 - m_2) \times L$$

$$L = \frac{P \times t}{(m_1 - m_2)}$$

In this case:
$$L = \frac{3 \times 1000 \times 300}{(m_1 - m_2)}$$

The accepted value for the specific latent heat of vaporisation of water is 2300000 J/kg.

G5 Atomic structure (1)

THE NUCLEAR ATOM

During the nineteenth century many ideas and theories were put forward concerning the structure of an atom. The model which was eventually accepted was called the **nuclear atom** and was based on the work of Ernest Rutherford and Neils Bohr. They suggested:

- an atom has a central core called the nucleus which contains small particles called **protons** and **neutrons**. Both particles have a relative atomic mass of one but the proton is positively charged whilst the neutron has no charge.

and

- Extremely small negatively charged particles called **electrons** orbit the nucleus at high speeds.

Particle	Position	Charge	Relative atomic mass
proton	in the nucleus	$+1$	1
neutron	in the nucleus	0	1
electron	outside the nucleus	-1	almost zero $\left(\frac{1}{1836}\right)$

Neutral atoms contain the same number of protons and electrons. This number is called the **proton number**. The number of protons and neutrons in the nucleus is called the **nucleon number**.

Using these ideas and the information contained in the *Periodic Table* it is possible to draw the atomic structure of different elements.

ATOMIC STRUCTURE AND THE PERIODIC TABLE

The Periodic Table contains information concerning the atomic structure of all known elements.

nucleon number 27 · **Al** · element's symbol
proton number 13

Group 1	Group 2					the transition metals							Group 3	4	5	6	7	0
																		$^{4}_{2}$He helium
							$^{1}_{1}$H hydrogen											
$^{7}_{3}$Li lithium	$^{9}_{4}$Be beryllium												$^{11}_{5}$B boron	$^{12}_{6}$C carbon	$^{14}_{7}$N nitrogen	$^{16}_{8}$O oxygen	$^{19}_{9}$F fluorine	$^{20}_{10}$Ne neon
$^{23}_{11}$Na sodium	$^{24}_{12}$Mg magnesium												$^{27}_{13}$Al aluminium	$^{28}_{14}$Si silicon	$^{31}_{15}$P phosphorus	$^{32}_{16}$S sulphur	$^{35\cdot5}_{17}$Cl chlorine	$^{40}_{18}$Ar argon
$^{39}_{19}$K potassium	$^{40}_{20}$Ca calcium	$^{45}_{21}$Sc scandium	$^{48}_{22}$Ti titanium	$^{51}_{23}$V vanadium	$^{52}_{24}$Cr chromium	$^{55}_{25}$Mn manganese	$^{56}_{26}$Fe iron	$^{59}_{27}$Co cobalt	$^{59}_{28}$Ni nickel	$^{64}_{29}$Cu copper	$^{65}_{30}$Zn zinc		$^{70}_{31}$Ga gallium	$^{73}_{32}$Ge germanium	$^{75}_{33}$As arsenic	$^{79}_{34}$Se selenium	$^{80}_{35}$Br bromine	$^{84}_{36}$Kr krypton
$^{85}_{37}$Rb rubidium	$^{88}_{38}$Sr strontium	$^{89}_{39}$Y yttrium	$^{91}_{40}$Zr zirconium	$^{93}_{41}$Nb niobium	$^{96}_{42}$Mo molybdenum	$^{98}_{43}$Tc technetium	$^{101}_{44}$Ru ruthenium	$^{103}_{45}$Rh rhodium	$^{106}_{46}$Pd palladium	$^{108}_{47}$Ag silver	$^{112}_{48}$Cd cadmium		$^{115}_{49}$In indium	$^{119}_{50}$Sn tin	$^{122}_{51}$Sb antimony	$^{128}_{52}$Te tellurium	$^{127}_{53}$I iodine	$^{131}_{54}$Xe xenon
$^{133}_{55}$Cs caesium	$^{137}_{56}$Ba barium	$^{139}_{57}$La lanthanum	$^{178.5}_{72}$Hf hafnium	$^{181}_{73}$Ta tantalum	$^{184}_{74}$W tungsten	$^{186}_{75}$Re rhenium	$^{190}_{76}$Os osmium	$^{192}_{77}$Ir iridium	$^{195}_{78}$Pt platinum	$^{197}_{79}$Au gold	$^{201}_{80}$Hg mercury		$^{204}_{81}$Tl thallium	$^{207}_{82}$Pb lead	$^{209}_{83}$Bi bismuth	$^{210}_{84}$Po polonium	$^{210}_{85}$At astatine	$^{222}_{86}$Rn radon
$^{223}_{37}$Fr francium	$^{226}_{88}$Ra radium	$^{227}_{89}$Ac actinium																

$^{140}_{58}$Ce cerium	$^{141}_{59}$Pr prae-sodymium	$^{144}_{60}$Nd rhenium	$^{147}_{61}$Pm promethium	$^{150}_{62}$Sm samarium	$^{152}_{63}$Eu europium	$^{157}_{64}$Gd gadolinium	$^{159}_{65}$Tb terbium	$^{162}_{66}$Dy dysprosium	$^{165}_{67}$Ho holmium	$^{167}_{68}$Er erbium	$^{169}_{69}$Tm thulium	$^{173}_{70}$Yb ytterbium	$^{175}_{71}$Lu lutecium
$^{232}_{90}$Th thorium	$^{231}_{91}$Pa protactinium	$^{238}_{92}$U uranium	$^{237}_{93}$Np neptunium	$^{242}_{94}$Pu plutonium	$^{243}_{95}$Am americium	$^{247}_{96}$Cm curium	$^{247}_{97}$Bk berkelium	$^{251}_{98}$Cf californium	$^{254}_{99}$Es einsteinium	$^{253}_{100}$Fm fermium	$^{256}_{101}$Md mendelevium	$^{254}_{102}$No nobelium	$^{257}_{103}$Lr lawrencium

Hydrogen is the first element in the table. It has a proton number of 1 so it contains one proton in its nucleus. Because the atom is neutral there must be just one electron orbiting the nucleus. Its nucleon number is also 1 so the nucleus contains (1–1) = no neutrons.

The second element in the table is helium. It has a proton number of 2 and contains 2 protons in its nucleus and has 2 orbiting electrons. Its nucleon number is 4 so the nucleus contains (4–2) = 2 neutrons.

The atomic structure of hydrogen

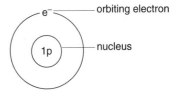

The atomic structure of helium

G6 Atomic structure (2)

CONTINUED FROM PAGE 61:

The third element in the table is lithium.
It has a proton number of 3 and contains 3 protons in its nucleus. It has 3 orbiting electrons. Its nucleon number is 7 so the nucleus contains (7–3) = 4 neutrons.
Electrons travel around the nucleus in orbits or shells. Each orbit can only contain a certain number of electrons. When an orbit is full any remaining electrons must go into the next empty outer orbit.

The first orbit can hold just 2 electrons.

The second orbit can hold up to 8 electrons.

The third orbit can hold up to 8 electrons.

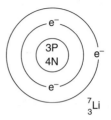

the atomic structure of lithium.

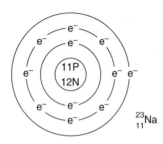

the atomic structure of sodium.

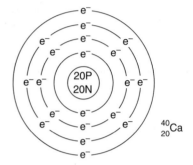

the atomic structure of calcium .

ISOTOPES

According to this model of an atom it is only possible to have whole number nucleon numbers. There are however some elements in the Periodic Table that seem to break this rule. Chlorine has a nucleon number of 35.5. Chlorine has a proton number of 17 and should therefore contain (35.5–17) = 18.5 neutrons

The solution to this problem came when it was discovered that these were two 'different' chlorine atoms.

One atom contained 17 protons and 18 neutrons in its nucleus. The second contained 17 protons and 20 neutrons in its nucleus.

When an element can have different numbers of neutrons in its nucleus, these different atoms are called **isotopes**. Isotopes of any one element are chemically identical. It is only in nuclear reactions any differences might occur.

The nucleon number which appears in the periodic table is an average. It takes into account the proportions of each isotope present in a normal sample. For chlorine in a normal sample three quarters of the atoms have a nucleon number of 35 whilst the remaining quarter have a nucleon number of 37. The average nucleon number is therefore 35.5.

Radioactive isotopes

Many elements, especially the heavier elements, in the Periodic Table have isotopes which are unstable and give out radioactive emissions. These atoms are described as being radioactive and are called **radioactive isotopes**.

Chlorine has two common isotopes ... chlorine-35 and chlorine -37

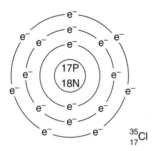

the atomic structure of chlorine-35

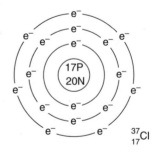

the atomic structure of chlorine-37

G7 Radioactivity

In 1896 Henri Becquerel found that a uranium salt he was experimenting with was emitting invisible rays which affected his photographic plates. He had discovered **radioactivity**. Scientists studying these rays agreed there were in fact three different types.

These were called **alpha** (α) **radiation**, **beta** (β) **radiation** and **gamma** (γ) **radiation**.

SUMMARY OF THE PROPERTIES OF ALPHA, BETA, AND GAMMA RADIATION

Type of radiation	α particles	β particles	γ rays
Nature	Particles consist of 2 protons and 2 neutrons. It has the same structure as a helium nucleus ${}^{4}_{2}$He.	Fast moving electrons with speeds up to $\frac{9}{10} \times$ the speed of light. (These are emitted from the nucleus **not** the electron orbits.)	Short wavelength electromagnetic radiation.
Charge	2^{+}	1^{-}	0
Mass	4	$\frac{1}{1836} \times$ that of a proton (almost negligible compared with an atom)	0
Penetrating power	Least penetrating radiation. It is **unable** to penetrate more than a few cm of air or one or two sheets of paper.	More penetrating than α but less penetrating than γ. It is stopped by thin sheets of aluminium (0.5 cm).	Most penetrating of all three types of radiation. Almost unaffected by air. Able to, travel through substantial thicknesses of lead (10 cm).
Ionising power (ability of radiation to displace electrons from an atom causing it to become ionized or charged)	Very strongly ionizing *Comparative figure* 100000	Less ionising than α but more ionising than γ. *Comparative figure* 1000	Least ionising of all three types of radiation. *Comparative figure* 1
Deflection by magnetic or electric fields	Deflected a little, in the opposite direction to β particles because of +ve charge	Deflected quite a lot, in the opposite direction to α particles because of –ve charge.	No deflection. Not affected by either type of field.
Detection	All three types of radiation can be detected using photographic film, cloud chambers, or Geiger-Müller tubes.		

G8 Radioactive decay

RADIOACTIVE PROCESSES

Atoms that are naturally radioactive have unstable nuclei. In order to become more stable they need to lose some mass and some energy. They do this by emitting alpha, beta and gamma radiation ie the atoms under go radioactive decay.

DECAY BY ALPHA EMISSION

$$^{226}_{88}\text{Ra} \longrightarrow ^{222}_{86}\text{Rn} + ^{4}_{2}\text{He}$$

radioactive material   new more stable nucleus   α particle

By emitting a particle composed of two protons and two neutrons (equivalent to a helium nucleus) a new lighter element with a more stable nucleus is produced.

DECAY BY BETA EMISSION

$$^{234}_{90}\text{Th} \longrightarrow ^{234}_{91}\text{Pa} + ^{0}_{1}\text{e}$$

β particle

When beta decay occurs, a neutron in the nucleus splits up to form a proton and an electron. This electron is emitted as a beta particle leaving an extra proton in the nucleus. A new more stable nucleus is created but with no change in atomic mass.

DECAY BY GAMMA EMISSION

After a nucleus has emitted an alpha or beta particle it may have an excess of energy which it needs to lose. It does so by emitting short wavelength radiation called gamma rays.

DECAY SERIES

By emitting a combination of alpha, beta, and gamma radiation atoms gradually change into new, lighter more stable elements. A set of equations that describe these changes is called a decay series.

$$^{238}_{92}\text{U} \longrightarrow ^{234}_{90}\text{Th} + ^{4}_{2}\text{He} + \gamma$$

$$^{234}_{90}\text{Th} \longrightarrow ^{234}_{91}\text{Pa} + ^{0}_{1}\text{e} + \gamma$$

BACKGROUND RADIATION

Radiation originating from
- rocks such as granite
- space
- human activities with radioactive materials and processes all contribute to what is called **background radiation**.

RATE OF DECAY

Some radioactive materials decay rapidly, giving off a large number of particles in a short period of time. Others decay extremely slowly, their radiation being much less intense. This rate of *radioactive decay is totally unaffected by physical conditions such as temperature and pressure.*

The average number of nuclei which decay in one second is called the **activity** and is measured in **becquerels** (Bq). A radioactive material which has an activity of 1 Bq is decaying on average at the rate of one nucleus /second.

(A second way of describing the rate of decay is by using the term **half-life**.)

HALF-LIFE

Suppose a sample of radioactive iodine-131 consists of 160 atoms. After 8 days half of these atoms will have decayed leaving 80 iodine-131 atoms. After a further 8 days half of these 80 will have decayed leaving 40 undecayed atoms. After a further 8 days half of these 40 will have decayed leaving just 20 of the original atoms unchanged. The rate of decay of the sample of iodine-131 is described by saying that it has a **half-life** of 8 days.

The half life of a radioactive isotope/atom is the time taken for half of its atoms to decay.

Table of half-lifes

Element/Isotope	Half life
Uranium-238	4.5×10^9 years
Radium-226	1620 years
Iodine-131	8 days
Radon-222	4 days
Radium-214	20 minutes
Polonium-212	3×10^{-7} s

HALF-LIFE GRAPHS

If a graph is plotted of the number of undecayed atoms against time for any radioactive isotope *it always has the characteristic shape shown below.*

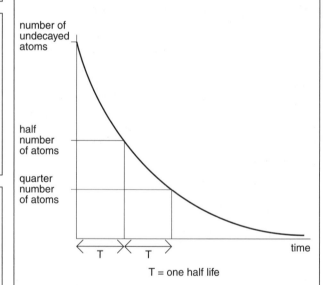

T = one half life

Random process

Radioactive decay is a random process. It is impossible to predict precisely when an atom is going to decay. *It is only possible to predict approximately how many atoms should decay over a period of time.*

G9 Radioactive isotopes

APPLICATIONS OF RADIOACTIVE ISOTOPES

Some elements, if they are bombarded with particles such as neutrons, alpha particles, or beta particles become radioactive, themselves. These new materials are called radioactive isotopes or **radio-isotopes**.

Radioactive tracers

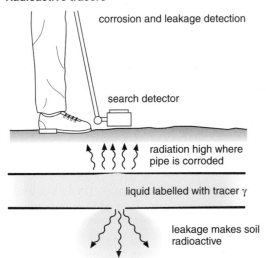

corrosion and leakage detection

search detector

radiation high where pipe is corroded

liquid labelled with tracer γ

leakage makes soil radioactive

Finding a leak in a pipe buried underground can be both expensive and time consuming. If however a radio-isotope which emits strong beta or gamma rays is added to the fluid in the pipe, increased levels of radioactivity in the ground near to the leak can be detected using sensitive radiation detectors.

Radioactive tracers are used in hospitals as a means of checking the flow of material through the body. Sodium-24 can be introduced into the blood stream to check for internal bleeding, iodine-131 can be used to check the function of the thyroid gland.

Phosphorous-32 is used by scientists in their search for better fertilisers. Some of the radio-isotope is included in the fertiliser being tested and the crop with which it is being fed is checked periodically to see how radioactive it has become. The better the fertiliser, the greater the amount taken in and the more radioactive will be the the plant. (*These* crops are not used for consumption.)

Quantity control

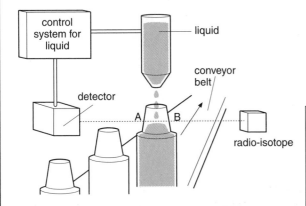

control system for liquid

liquid

detector

conveyor belt

A   B

radio-isotope

In order not to waste any of this product the amount of fluid put into each bottle is controlled by a radio-isotope and a detector. Whilst the detector is receiving particles from the source, liquid is allowed to flow into the bottle. When the liquid reaches level AB it prevents the particles reaching the detector so the control systems stops the flow of liquid into the bottle. Using a system such as this prevents the bottles from being under or over-filled.

Quality control

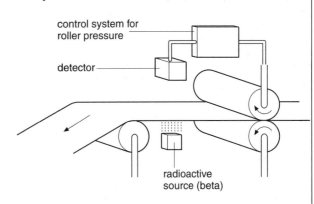

control system for roller pressure

detector

radioactive source (beta)

Paper manufacturers use radio-isotopes as part of their production quality control.

If the paper becomes too thin the number of beta particles reaching the detector increases. The control system recognises this and decreases the pressure between the rollers. If the paper becomes too thick the number of beta particles reaching the detector decreases and the control system increases the pressure between the rollers. This constant monitoring of the thickness improves the efficiency of the process.

If the radio-isotope is changed for one which emits beta particles the same control system could be used by a firm producing sheet metal.

Radiotherapy

Cobalt-60 is a radio-isotope which emits gamma rays. This radiation, in limited doses, can be used to kill cancerous cells and treat tumours.

Sterilisation

Gamma radiation can be used to sterilise medical equipment as it kills any bacteria that are present.

Food preservation

Food goes bad and begins to rot because of the presence of microbes. If food is irradiated with gamma rays these microbes are killed and the food can be stored for a much longer period of time.

Carbon dating

All living things have inside them the naturally occurring radio-isotope carbon-14. When they die the amount of carbon-14 in their bodies begins to decrease because of radioactive decay. The half-life of carbon-14 is 5730 years. By measuring the levels of carbon-14 remaining in a piece of wood or cloth or a body, it is possible to determine the age of the item.

THE DANGERS OF RADIOACTIVITY

All three types of radioactivity can be beneficial; but because of the genetic damage that each of them can cause to tissue cells it is essential that radioactive materials are used correctly. There are strict guidelines for the handling of radioactive sources.

In schools, pupils are not allowed to handle radioactive sources.

People working with radioactive sources are often required to wear special clothing or use lead shields to protect them from radiation. Badges which detect radiation are also worn and at the end of each day they are checked to discover how much radiation each worker has been exposed to.

G10 Nuclear power

FISSION

Under certain circumstances it is possible to make a stable atom unstable. For example, if an additional neutron is 'pushed into' the nucleus of an atom it may become so unstable, that rather than emitting alpha, beta or gamma rays it may completely break apart. This process is called **nuclear fission** and is the basis of the nuclear bomb and the energy source of nuclear power stations.

$$^{235}_{92}U + {}^{1}_{0}n \longrightarrow {}^{236}_{92}U \longrightarrow \text{2 new elements} + 3{}^{1}_{0}n + \text{energy}$$

If a neutron is absorbed into the nucleus of a uranium-235 atom, it becomes unstable and breaks apart producing two new lighter elements, some fast moving neutrons and a lot of energy which had been used to hold the nucleus together (binding energy).

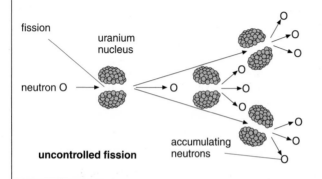

uncontrolled fission

The neutrons ejected from the broken nucleus may be absorbed by other uranium-235 atoms whose nuclei will split releasing even more neutrons and energy. If this chain reaction continues to accelerate too much energy is released too quickly resulting in a nuclear explosion.

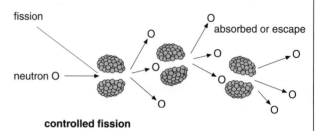

controlled fission

The energy released from a single uranium-235 nucleus when it breaks apart is extremely large. If the chain reaction could be controlled it would be an invaluable source of energy.

In nuclear power stations, the rate at which this reaction takes place and energy released is adjusted by control rods. These are positioned inside the nuclear reactor to absorb approximately two out of every three neutrons produced in the reaction. Under these circumstances the chain reaction will neither accelerate or decelerate but will just " tick,over".

THE ADVANCED GAS-COOLED NUCLEAR REACTOR

The fuel rods contain pure uranium-235

The energy released by the fission reaction is carried from the core by a gas such as carbon dioxide under high pressure to heat exchangers. Here water is heated producing high-pressure steam which is then used to drive the turbines which generate the electricity.

The control rods contain boron which absorb some of the ejected neutrons so that the reaction can be controlled.

The ejected neutrons have velocities which are too high for many of them to be captured and absorbed by the uranium-235 nuclei. Rods containing a **moderator** which slows down the neutrons so that they can be more easily captured are placed within the core. Graphite is commonly used here.

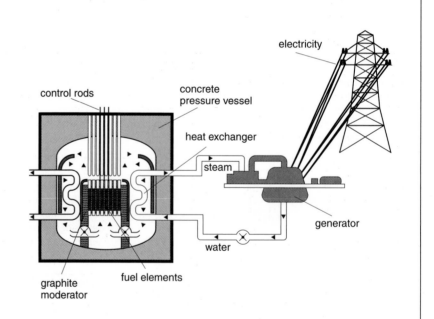

FUSION

Most of our energy here on Earth comes from the Sun. This energy is produced by a different kind of nuclear reaction called **nuclear fusion**. In a fusion reaction the nuclei of light elements join together to produce more stable, heavier elements.

$$^{2}_{1}H + {}^{2}_{1}H \longrightarrow {}^{3}_{2}He + {}^{1}_{0}n + \text{energy}$$

Unfortunately because of the extremely high temperatures and pressures needed to produce this reaction scientists have so far been unable to tap into this source of energy.

H1 The Solar System

The Earth is one of nine known **planets** which orbit the Sun. These, together with other bodies called **moons**, **asteroids**, and **comets** make up our **Solar System**. The positions and movements of all the bodies in the Solar System are determined by gravitational forces.

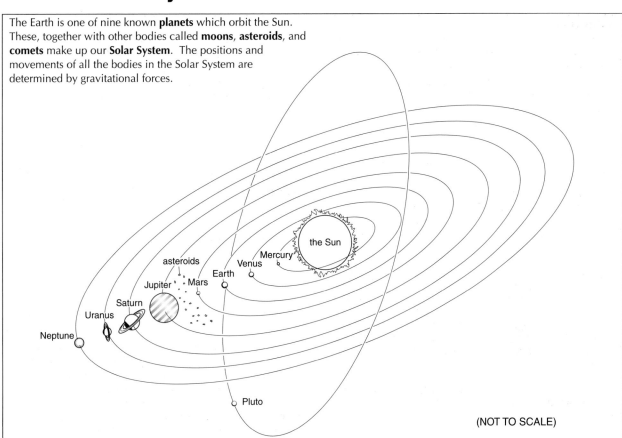

(NOT TO SCALE)

Planet	Average distance from Sun (millions of km)	Time to orbit Sun (years)	Time to rotate about axis (h)	Relative mass	Relative surface gravity	Average surface temperature (°C)	Number of moons
Mercury	58	0.24	1416	0.05	0.37	350	0
Venus	108	0.6	5832	0.81	0.89	460	0
Earth	150	1	24	1.0	1.00	17	1
Mars	228	1.9	24.6	0.11	0.38	−25	2
Jupiter	779	11.9	10	318.0	2.6	−120	16
Saturn	1430	29.5	10.5	95.0	1.15	−180	21
Uranus	2870	84	10.8	14.0	1.60	−210	15
Neptune	4496	165	15.8	17.5	1.43	−220	8
Pluto	5906	248	154	0.003	?	−240	1

The **Sun** is our nearest star. It is an M class yellow dwarf. It is the main source of energy within the Solar System. Nuclear fusion gives rise to temperatures of several million degrees Celsius in the Sun's core. Its surface temperature is approximately 6000 °C.

The **planets** of a solar system are the non-luminous bodies which orbit the star at its centre. In our solar system the nine known planets are (from the Sun outwards): Mercury, Venus, Earth, Mars, Jupiter, Saturn, Uranus, Neptune, and Pluto. (**M**any **V**ery **E**nergetic **M**en **J**og **S**lowly **U**p to **N**ewport **P**agnell). All of the planets orbit the Sun in the same plane (except Pluto) and travel in the same direction around the Sun.

Asteroids are large pieces of rock between Mars and Jupiter which are orbiting the Sun. The largest asteroids are over 200 km in diameter, whilst the smallest are only a few kilometres across.

Comets are bodies of rock and ice which orbit the Sun in a completely different plane to the planets. The most famous of these is Halley's comet which is visible from the Earth every 76 years.

A **moon** is a natural body which orbits a planet.

A **day** is the time it takes for a planet to rotate once about its axis. A day on Earth is 24 h but a day on Jupiter is just 10 h.

A **year** is the time it takes for a planet to orbit the Sun once. A year on Earth is, naturally enough, 1 Earth year but a year on Jupiter is 11.9 Earth years.

H2 Earth and space

THE EARTH

A day is the time it takes the Earth to rotate once about its axis (24 hours). For some of this time part of the Earth's surface will be facing the Sun. Here it will be **daytime**. For those places on the opposite side of the Earth that are not receiving light it will be **night-time**.

Because of the rotation of the Earth the Sun during the daytime, and the stars at night, appear to travel across the sky. The Sun appears to rise in the East, set in the West and is at its highest in the southern sky at noon.

The axis about which the Earth rotates is not perpendicular to the plane of its orbit. The axis is slightly tilted. This tilting gives rise to two very important effects:

- the difference in the number of hours of daylight in the summer and the winter
- the Seasons

light from the sun

When the North Pole of the Earth is tilted away from the Sun its heat and light are spread out over a large area giving rise to cooler and dimmer days in the northern hemisphere – winter. When the North Pole is tilted towards the Sun the energy the northern hemisphere receives is less spread out so the days are warmer and brighter. It is summer in this part of the world. The Earth moves around the Sun once every 365 days.

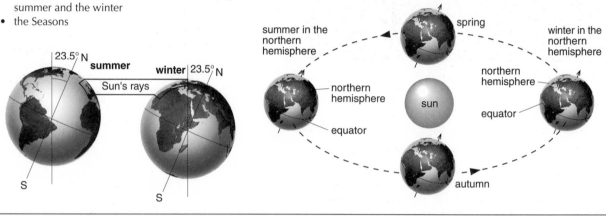

THE MOON

The Moon is the natural satellite of the Earth. It orbits the Earth every 28 days at a distance of approximately 384000 km. The Moon is held in orbit by the gravitational attraction between it and the Earth.

This gravitational attraction is also largely responsible for the periodic motions of our oceans (tides).

As the Moon passes over the oceans it 'pulls' the water causing a slight bulge. This is a *high tide*. Between the high tides when the gravitational attraction is smallest there is a *low tide*. Because the Earth is rotating there are at any point on the Earth's surface two high tides and two low tides every 24 hours.

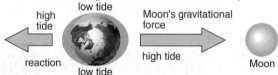

Phases of the moon

The Moon does not emit any light of its own. It is seen in the night sky because of the light it reflects from the Sun. The shape of the moon, as seen from the Earth, appears to change over a period of 28 days. This is due to the relative positions of the Earth, Moon, and Sun.

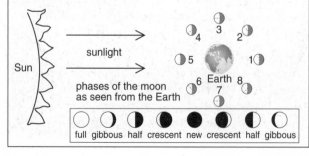

ARTIFICIAL SATELLITES

Artificial satellites can be put in orbit around the Earth. They may be used for:

- communications such as radio, television, telephones

- monitoring conditions on the Earth such as the weather, early warning of the movement of hurricanes.

- making observations of the universe without the interference of the Earth's atmosphere

  The Hubble telescope provides far better photographs of objects in space than any telescope sited on the Earth.

To be of continuous use communication satellites need to remain above the same place on the Earth. To achieve this the satellites are put into a **high geostationary orbit** above the equator. Satellites which monitor whole world conditions are put into **low polar orbits** which allow them to scan the surface as the planet rotates below.

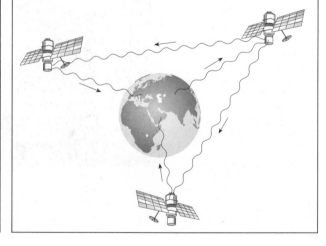

H3 Stars and the Universe

STARS AND THE SUN

The Sun is just one of approximately 100000 million stars in our galaxy, the Milky Way. A galaxy is a cluster of stars, dust, and gas held together by the forces of gravity.

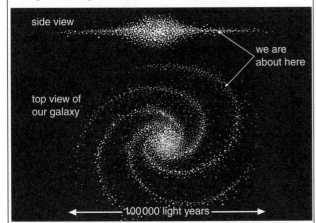

The distances between stars are so enormous they are measured in **light years**. One light year is the distance light can travel in one year. (Light can travel 300000 km in just one second.) Our nearest star after the Sun is Proxima Centauri which is 4.3 light years away.

In the known Universe there at at least a billion galaxies.

Life of a star

Stars are formed in space where sufficiently large amounts of dust and gases are pulled together by gravitational forces to cause the temperature at the core of this mass to increase in temperature and nuclear fusion between hydrogen atoms to take place. When the gravitational forces trying to pull the matter even closer is balanced by the expansive forces due to the very high temperatures the star enters its main **stable period** which can last for billions of years. Our Sun is at this stage now.

What happens next depends upon the mass of the star.

After the *stable period* there is no hydrogen left for the fusion reaction. Yellow dwarf stars like our Sun begin a second fusion reaction with helium nuclei reacting to produce carbon. At the same time the star expands and becomes a little cooler. The star is now a **red giant**. Later when the forces again become unbalanced the star contracts under the forces of gravity producing a **white dwarf** containing matter millions of times denser then that found on the Earth. As the white dwarf cools down it consequently changes colour, becoming first a red dwarf and ultimately a black dwarf.

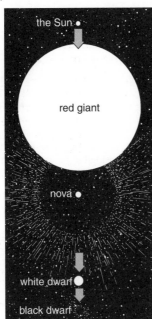

If the mass of a star is much larger than our Sun it may form a red supergiant which will become unstable and explode throwing dust and gases into the surrounding space. Such an exploding star is called a *supernova*. A very dense *neutron star* or *black hole* may be left.

ORIGINS OF THE UNIVERSE
Red-shift

As a train passes through a station or a racing car is driven towards and then past a spectator at high speed there is a noticeable change in the frequency of the sound heard as it passes and speeds away. Only the spectator hears this apparent change, to the driver the pitch of the engine is constant. The apparent drop in frequency is caused because the train and car are moving away rapidly. This phenomenon is called the **Doppler effect**. With special appparatus this can be observed with light waves.

Light from stars shows this effect, the light emitted being redder than it should be. It is known as **red-shift**. This indicates that stars are speeding away from the Earth.

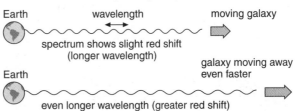

Even more interesting is that the further away a star or galaxy is the greater the red-shift is and the faster they are moving away from the Earth.

A similar pattern to this is seen when an object explodes.

- Every fragment of the object is moving away from every other fragment

- Those fragments that are moving most rapidly will be furthest from the site of the explosion.

The **Big Bang Theory of the Universe**, on the basis of this evidence, proposes that the Universe started many thousands of millions of years ago as one large mass which subsequently exploded.

A second theory suggests that at some stage in the future the forces of gravity will halt the expansion of the Universe and then begin to draw the matter back to its point of origin. At which point the whole process may well begin again. This is called the **Pulsating Universe**.

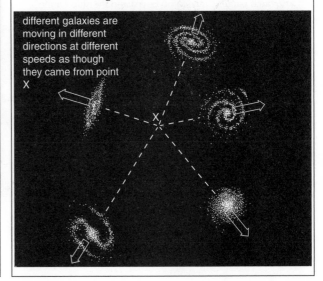

different galaxies are moving in different directions at different speeds as though they came from point X

H4 Floating and flying

FLOATING

If an object such as a beach ball is pushed under water it experiences a force trying to push it upwards. This force is called an **upthrust** and is created by the water which is pushed aside (**displaced**) by the ball as it is immersed.

Objects with large volumes will displace a large volume of water and so create a large upthrust. Small, compact objects will displace little water and so create small upthrusts.

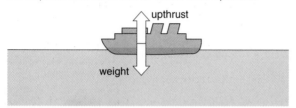

This ship is floating because the water it is displacing creates an upthrust equal to its weight.

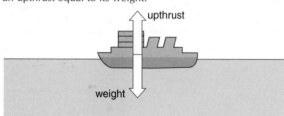

If the ship becomes heavier)loaded with cargo) it will sink lower, displacing more water until its upthrust is equal to its new weight.

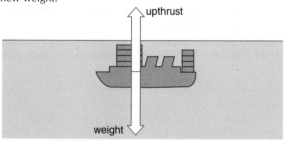

If too much cargo is loaded on board and the ship cannot displace enough water to create an upthrust equal to its weight the ship will sink.

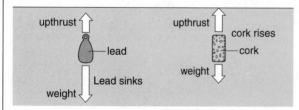

Objects which are light for their size (have a low **density**), such as a cork or a piece of polystyrene, when immersed in water will create an upthrust greater than their weight and so when released they will rise to the surface.

Submarines use these ideas. When they wish to submerge they fill tanks with water to gain enough weight to overcome their upthrust. When they wish to surface they pump this water out, lose weight and so rise.

FLYING

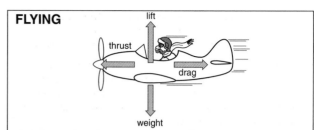

As an aircraft flies through the air it experiences four main forces. These are:

- **thrust**   This is the force which comes from the engines and drives the aircraft forwards

- **drag**   This is the force which resists the forward motion of the aircraft and is caused by air resistance. To keep this force to a minimum aircraft are designed with a streamlined shape.

- **weight**   This is the gravitational force of attraction acting downwards. To keep this to a minimum, strong light materials such as aluminium and carbon fibre are used in the construction of aircraft.

- **lift**   This is the force which pushes an aircraft upwards. It arises because of **Bernoulli's effect**.

When air is blown gently over a sheet of paper it will rise. An Italian scientist named Daniel Bernoulli was the first to explain why this happens. He discovered that the pressure of air, when it was flowing smoothly, changed as its velocity changed. The faster the air moved (*without becoming turbulent*) the lower the pressure became. As a consequence of this there is a pressure difference between the topside and the underside of the sheet of paper. This pressure difference gives rise to a lifting force.

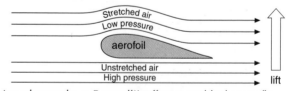

Aeroplanes rely on Bernoulli's effect to enable them to fly. The wings of all aircraft are specially shaped so that air flowing over the top of the wing is made to move faster than that passing below it. If the lift created by this pressure difference is large enough the aircraft will fly through the air.

Stalling is the onset of turbulent flow due to a *too high angle of attack*.

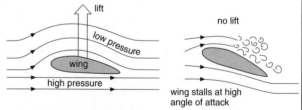

Stalling can be caused by:
- the aircraft not moving through the air fast enough to create the necessary lift.

- the angle of the wing causing turbulent flow over the wing.

Questions

The **Multiple choice** and the **Short answer/Structured questions** are arranged and numbered according to the Contents listing. There are no **Free response/Long questions**.

QUESTION REFERENCES: Each question has been given a **Reference** under the question number. The purpose of these **References** is to help you identify and chose questions from a particular area of the syllabus. This is especially useful if you want to revise specific topics only.

For example, the **Reference** for multiple choice question number 1 is:

1.
(FAC)

the **first letter** (F) is the *Tier* indicator (F = foundation H= higher)

the **third letter** (C) is for the *multiple choice questions;* the answer letter (A, B, C or D)

the **second letter** (A) is the Chapter indicator
(A = energy
B = heat
C= motion etc)

Question 1 is therefore a **Foundation question** from **Chapter A** (energy) **(and the multiple choice answer is choice C)**.

Note: numerical answers for the Short answer/Structured questions are given separately at the end of this section.

QUESTION COVERAGE: no attempt has been made to cover every aspect of every syllabus. You will not find questions from both tiers from every part of all the syllabuses. The selection of questions has been made to reasonably represent the syllabuses available and to enable you to assess your own subject strengths and weaknesses.

EXAMINATION TIER: these are indicated:

F - *foundation* (GCSE grades G-C)

H - *higher* (GCSE grades D-A*)

ANSWER SPACES: the answer spaces have generally been omitted from the **Short answer/Structured questions** section.

ANSWERS: all answers are provided by the author.

Multiple Choice:

1C, 2D, 3A, 4 B, 5D, 6D, 7B, 8D, 9C, 10D, 11A, 12D, 13C, 14D, 15B, 16B, 17B, 18C, 19B, 20C, 21A, 22B, 23D, 24A, 25D

Short answer/Structured questions:

1(a)(i) 22000 J, (a)(ii) 440 W, 4(a)(iii) 2.67 m/s2, (c)(i) 20 cm2, 5(a)(i) 3.5 m/s, (ii) 300, (iii) 0.5 m/s2, (iv) 30 N, 6(b) 0,2 m/s, 7(b) 2.5 m/s2, 8(a)(i) 25 N/cm2, (ii) 25 N/cm2, (iii) 2500 N, 9(c)(iii) 1360 m, 14(a)(ii) 0.82 A, (iii) 14.4 Ω, 48 Ω, 1(b)(ii) 8.9 Ω, 15(a)(ii) 9 V, 16(a)(ii) 1.5 C, (c)(i) 1200, (ii) 3 600 000 J, (iii) 4320 MJ, (d) 0.01 Ω mm, 20(b)(ii)(2) 2.5 hours, 21(c)(ii) 6 hours, 22(b)(iii) 28000 km/h

---

Multiple choice questions

1. The diagram shows a crane lifting a load of 30 000 N
(FAC) through a distance of 10 metres.

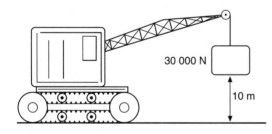

How much useful work does the crane do on the load?
A 3 000 J
B 3 000 N/m
C 300 000 J
D 300 000 N

2. Which of these (**A, B, C** or **D**) involves most power?
(HAD) A a force of 10 N moving 10 m in 10 s
B a force of 20 N moving 5 m in 10 s
C a force of 10 N moving 5 m in 5 s
D a force of 10 N moving 10 m in 5 s

3. A car is travelling on a level road. The driver has to
(FCA) stop quickly.
Which of these (**A, B, C** or **D**) has the greatest effect on the stopping distance?
A the kinetic energy of the car
B the potential energy of the car
C the straightness of the road
D how far the driver can see

4. A skier is sliding down a slope at a steady speed.
(FCB) Which of the following is true?

A there are no forces on the skier
B the forces on the skier are balanced
C there is an unbalanced force downwards
D there is an unbalanced force along the slope

5.
(HCD) A constant force acts on an object. If there is no friction, which of these velocity (v) – time (t) graphs (**A, B, C** or **D**) shows the motion of the object?

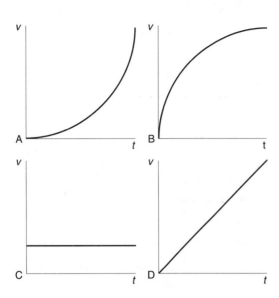

6.
(FDD) The four objects **A, B, C** and **D** all have the same weight. Which one produces the greatest pressure on the bench?

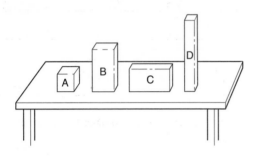

7.
(HDB) Which of these (**A, B, C** or **D**) depends on the atmosphere exerting pressure?
A a ball falling to the ground
B drinking through a straw
C the spray from a can of cola
D bath water emptying down a plug hole

8.
(FED) Here is a diagram of a wave.

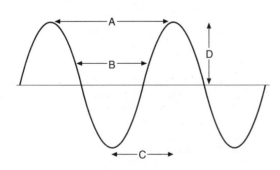

Which letter (**A, B, C** or **D**) shows the amplitude?

9.
(FEC) One of these diagrams (**A, B, C** or **D**) shows what happens when a vertical ray of light is reflected by a mirror. Which one is it?

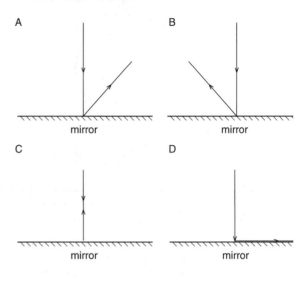

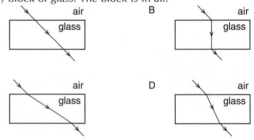

10.
(HED) Here are some statements about electromagnetic waves.
1 they all travel through a vacuum
2 they all travel with the same velocity in any one medium
3 they all carry energy from one place to another
Which of these statements (choose **A, B, C** or **D**) is correct?
A 1 only
B 1 and 2 only
C 2 and 3 only
D 1, 2 and 3

11.
(HEA) When viewing a total eclipse of the Sun, an observer on the Earth passes into the shadow of the Moon. At this instant the observer can deduce that
A heat (IR) and light travel at the same speed
B light waves can be diffracted
C light waves can interfere to give darkness
D white light is made up of different colours

12.
(HED) The ray diagrams show a ray of light passing through a block of glass. The block is in air.

Which of these (**A, B, C** or **D**) is correct?

13.
(HFC) A coil of wire is rotated in a permanent magnetic field. Which of these (**A, B, C** or **D**) will happen?
A the coil starts to rotate on its own
B the magnetic field reduces to zero
C an electric current is produced
D the magnet starts to rotate

14.
(HED) Which of these statements (**A, B, C** or **D**) about ultraviolet light (UV) is **NOT** true?
A it makes some materials fluoresce
B it can cause tanning of the skin
C it is emitted by the Sun
D it travels faster than visible light

15.
(FFB) Look at the diagram of an electric plug.

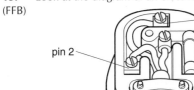

Which of these (**A, B, C** or **D**) is correct?

	The wire to pin 1 is	The wire to pin 2 is
A	live	yellow/green
B	earth	blue
C	neutral	brown
D	earth	brown

16.
(FFB) Jean is using an electric grass cutter which should have a 10 A (amperes) fuse fitted in its plug. It has been wrongly fitted with a 3 A fuse. The grass cutter will
A operate normally
B blow the fuse
C cut more slowly
D cut more quickly

17.
(FFB) Which of these (**A, B, C** or **D**) shows two lamps in parallel with the cell (battery)?

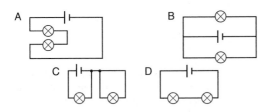

18.
(FFC) Which of these (**A, B, C** or **D**) shows a correctly wired ammeter and voltmeter?

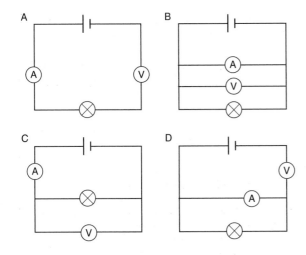

19.
(FFB) We measure the electricity used at home in kilowatt hours and not joules because:
A kilowatt hours measure power
B kilowatt hours are larger units
C joules measure power
D joules are larger units

20.
(FFC) Giles has a 2 kW electric fire. The meter shows that there is only 3 kWh of electricity left. How long can Giles have his fire on? Is it
A 40 minutes
B 1 hour
C 1 hour 30 minutes
D 6 hours

21.
(FFA) Sarah built this circuit.

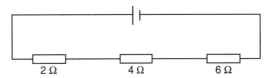

Which of these (**A, B, C** or **D**) gives the total resistance, in ohms, of the resistors?
A $2 + 4 + 6$
B $2 \times 4 \times 6$
C $\frac{1}{2} + \frac{1}{4} + \frac{1}{6}$
D $12 / (2 + 4 + 6)$

22.
(FFB) The circuits shown below are made from the same batteries and lamps.

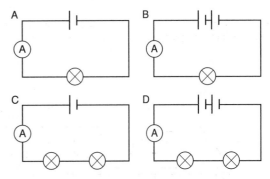

In which circuit (**A, B, C** or **D**) is the current the greatest?

23.
(HFD) A 20 ohm resistor has a current of 4 amps flowing through it. What is the potential difference (voltage) across the resistor?
A 0.2 volts
B 5 volts
C 24 volts
D 80 volts

24.
(HFA) Wayne is designing a control system for a tropical fish tank heater. The system uses a 240 V (volt) supply and has an internal resistance of 240 Ω (ohms). Which of these fuses should he fit into the system?
A 3 amp fuse
B 5 amp fuse
C 10 amp fuse
D 13 amp fuse

25.
(HGD) A material is used to make electrical fuses. Which property is essential for its use?
A bad conductor of electricity
B high boiling point
C high density
D low melting point

Short Answer/Structured Questions

1.
(FA)
A skier is pulled up a slope by holding a handle attached to a moving cable.
The cable passes round pulleys at the top and bottom of the slope.
The pulleys are driven by an electric motor.

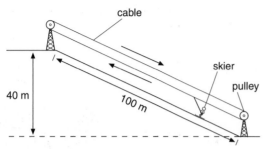

(a) The skier weighs 550 N. She travels 100 m along the slope and rises a vertical height of 40 m.
  (i) Calculate the useful work done (joules) just to lift the skier to the top of the slope. [3]
  (ii) The skier takes 50 s to travel up the slope.

  Use power = $\dfrac{\text{work done}}{\text{time taken}}$ to calculate the power needed just to <u>lift her</u> to the top of the slope.

  power: _____ unit: _____ [3]

(b) The power output of the motor is greater than the power needed just to lift the skier to the top of the slope.
Give **two** reasons for this. [2]
(MEG Sp)

2.
(HA)
(a) Wind energy is an example of renewable energy.
Give **three** other examples of renewable energy. [3]

(b) Most of the energy available to us originated in the Sun. Explain how some of the Sun's energy has become the energy which is now stored in coal. You should name the process and the type of energy involved at each stage. [6]
(SEG Sp)

3.
(HB)
(a) The following diagram shows a solar panel used to heat water.

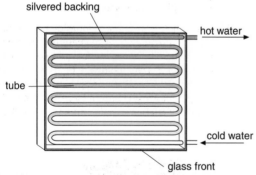

  (i) Name the process by which energy is transferred:
    1. from the Sun to the tube in the panel [1]
    2. from the tube to the water [1]
  (ii) Which of the following would be the most suitable material for the tube containing the water?
    black plastic
    copper painted black
    frosted glass
    polished stainless steel [1]
  (iii) Give TWO reasons for your choice in part (ii). [2]
(London Examinations Sp)

4.
(FC)
(a) Peter cycles from home to school. The following graph represents the journey.

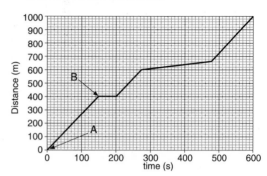

  (i) During the journey Peter has to stop at traffic lights and to cycle up a steep hill. Apart from this he travels at a constant speed. Redraw the graph and on it:
    1. write a letter 'L' where Peter is stopped at the traffic lights;
    2. write a letter 'H' where Peter is cycling up the steep hill. [2]
  (ii) How far is it from Peter's home to school? [1]
  (iii) Calculate Peter's speed (m/s) between points **A** and **B**. [2]

(b) The following diagram shows the shape of the rear tyre on Peter's bicycle when he is not sitting on it.

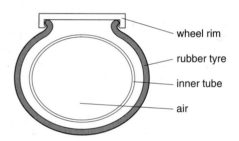

  (i) Draw a similar diagram to show the shape of the tyre when Peter sits on his bicycle. [1]
  (ii) Which of the following words best describes the forces which change the shape of the tyre when Peter sits on his bicycle?
    bending compressing stretching twisting [1]
  (iii) In the past, bicycle tyres were made of solid rubber.

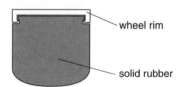

  Explain why air-filled tyres are preferred to solid rubber tyres. [2]

(c) The combined weight of Peter and his bicycle is 600 N. This weight is divided equally over each of the two wheels. Each tyre is in contact with the road through a strip 10 cm by 2 cm.
  (i) Calculate the area (cm²) of each tyre in contact with the road. [1]
(London Examinations Sp)

5.
(HC)
(a) Peter cycles from home to school. The following graph represents the journey.

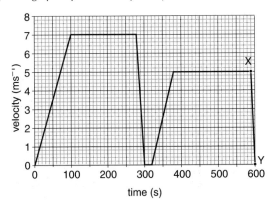

time (s)

(i) What is Peter's velocity after 50 s? [1]
(ii) After how many seconds does Peter stop at some traffic lights? [1]
(iii) Calculate Peter's deceleration, in m/s², between points **X** and **Y**. [2]
(iv) Peter and his bicycle have a combined mass of 60 kg. Calculate the resultant force exerted on Peter and his bicycle as he decelerates between points **X** and **Y**. [2]

(b) **(i)** After his journey, Peter noticed that his bicycle tyres, and the air they contained, were warm. Explain why. [1]
(ii) Explain what effect, if any, this has on the force exerted on the walls of the tyres. [2]
(London Examinations Sp)

6.
(HC)
Two students hired a boat on a lake at their local park. The boat was tied loosely to a landing stage. It was not moving. One student threw a sports bag directly towards the other student who was standing upright in the boat waiting to catch it.

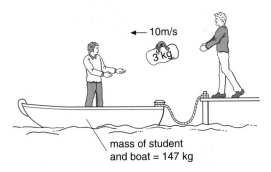

mass of student and boat = 147 kg

(a) Describe what will happen when the student in the boat catches the bag.
Explain your answer. [2]

(b) Calculate the speed of the boat after the student catches the bag. [3]

(c) Calculate the total kinetic energy before and after the student catches the bag.
before _____ after _____ [5]

(d) Account for any difference between these results. [2]
(MEG Sp)

7. A car has a mass of 1000 kilograms and it is moving along a straight road. There is a difference of 2500 newtons between the force from the engine acting to push the car forward and the forces acting to hold the car back.

(a) Name one force which will be acting to hold the car back. [1]

(b) Calculate the acceleration of the car. Include in your answer the equation you are going to use. Show clearly how you get to your final answer and give the unit. [3]

(c) At the top speed of the car, the force from the engine will not make the car go any faster. Why is this? [1]
(SEG Sp)

8.
(HD)

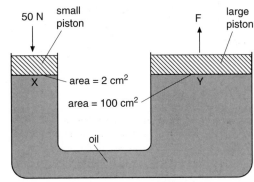

The diagram above shows the principle of the hydraulic car jack. A small force applied to the small piston enables a large load (the car) to be lifted by the large piston.

(a) **(i)** If a force of 50N is applied to the small piston, calculate the pressure measured in N/cm² produced in the oil at X. [2]
(ii) What is the pressure exerted by the oil at Y? [1]
(iii) Calculate the upward force, F, acting on the large piston. [1]

(b) Why does having air trapped in a hydraulic system make it less effective? [1]
(WJEC Sp)

9.
(FE)
(a) The cone of a loudspeaker moves when it is making a sound. How does the movement of the cone of the loudspeaker change when the following takes place?
(i) The loudness of the sound is increased. [2]
(ii) The pitch of the sound is increased. [2]

(b) A new motorway is built alongside a housing estate. A strong wire fence keeps the children from getting onto the motorway but people living on the estate find that the motorway traffic noise makes life less pleasant. They set up a committee to seek changes. The first change they seek is the building of a high wall between the motorway and the estate.

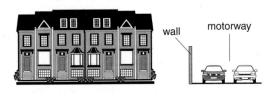

(i) State and explain how the wall will reduce the noise problem. [2]
(ii) State **one** change that could be made to the house in order to reduce the problem. [2]

(c) The diagram below illustrates the plan of an experiment to be carried out on a school trip to the Grand Canyon.

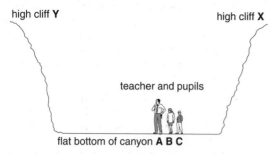

high cliff **Y**   high cliff **X**

teacher and pupils

flat bottom of canyon **A B C**

The teacher and his two pupils are standing close together in the bottom of the canyon.
- The teacher **A** is to fire a starting pistol.
- The pupils **B** and **C** are to both start clocks at the moment the teacher fires the pistol.
- Two echoes are expected to be heard by these pupils a short time later.
- Pupil **C** is to stop his watch when the first echo is heard.
- Pupil **B** is to stop her watch when the second echo is heard.

(i) Explain how the first echo is made and then heard by the pupils. [3]

(ii) Why would a second echo be expected? [2]

(iii) The speed of sound in air is 340 m/s. If echoes were heard 3 s and 5 s after the pistol was fired how far was cliff X (see diagram) from cliff Y? Show how you get your answer. [5]

(d) Explain clearly the difference between longitudinal and transverse waves.
Give **one** example of each. [6]

(e) A model boat is floating at rest in the centre of a pond. A large stone falls into the pond causing strong ripples to move out towards the boat.

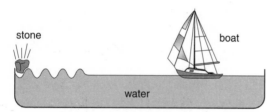

stone   boat

water

(i) What happens to the boat when the ripples reach it? [2]

(ii) What indicates that the boat has kinetic energy? [2]

(iii) What type of energy does the boat gain when it rises? [2]

(NICCEA Sp)

10.
(HE) (a) Ultrasonic waves are longitudinal waves.
(i) What does **ultrasonic** mean? [1]
(ii) What does **longitudinal** mean? [1]
(iii) The waves travel through carbon dioxide more slowly than through air. How do the frequency and the wavelength change when ultrasonic waves pass from air to carbon dioxide? [2]

(b) A small microphone is used with an oscilloscope to

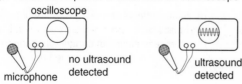

oscilloscope

no ultrasound   ultrasound
microphone detected   detected

A source which produces ultrasonic waves is placed about half a metre from a large metal sheet. The sheet has a small gap in it.

source   metal sheet

How would you use this apparatus to show that the ultrasonic waves are being diffracted.? [3]
(MEG Sp)

11.
(HE)

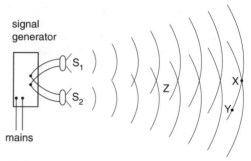

signal generator

S₁

S₂

mains   Z   X   Y

The diagram above shows the compression of sound waves from two identical loudspeakers. The compressions are spreading out and overlapping. State and explain:

(a) (i) why a loud sound is heard at X; [2]
(ii) why no sound would be heard at Y; [2]
(iii) what would be heard at Z. [2]

(b) What is meant by a longitudinal wave? [1]
(WJEC Sp)

12.
(FF) This shows part of the main wiring in a house.

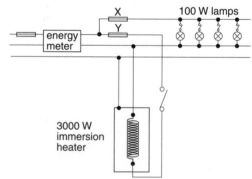

X   100 W lamps
Y
energy meter
3000 W immersion heater

(a) Why is fuse **X** rated at 5 A but fuse **Y** at 30 A? [2]

(b) Explain what might cause the fuse labelled **X** to melt. [2]

(c) Why are the lamps connected in parallel rather than in series? [2]

(d) The cable to the immersion heater has an Earth wire in it.
Explain how this Earth wire improves safety. [2]
(MEG Sp)

13.
(HF) Study the diagram below and read the following passage carefully before answering the questions.

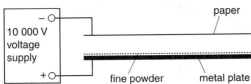

A fingerprint on the surface of a piece of paper can be revealed using electrostatically charged paper. The piece of paper is connected to the negative terminal of a 10 000 V supply. The metal plate coated with a fine powder is given a charge from this supply. The powder particles are repelled from the metal plate towards the paper. When they strike the paper they lose their charge before picking up another charge which causes them to be repelled back towards the plate. However, particles which strike the ridges of the fingerprint stick to them. This enables the fingerprint to be clearly seen.

(a) What is the charge on the powder when it leaves the plate? [1]

(b) Explain why the powder is repelled from the plate. [1]

(c) Explain in terms of *electrons* what happens when the particles come into contact with the paper. [2]
(WJEC Sp)

14.
(HF) **(a)** Mrs. Murphy has just bought three lamps for use outside in the garden. Each lamp will be at normal brightness when the voltage across its terminal is 12 V. Each lamp is to be wired so that it can be switched on and off independently of the others. A fourth switch, called the master control switch, will allow Mrs. Murphy to switch off all the lamps at once if a fault occurs.
(i) Draw a circuit diagram to show how the lamps are to be wired up to the switches and the power supply unit. The symbol for the power supply unit is shown for you. [7]

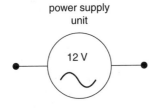

power supply
unit

(ii) Each lamp is marked 10 W, 12 V. Calculate the current flowing in each lamp when it is at normal brightness. Show clearly how you obtain your answer. [6]
(iii) Calculate the resistance of the filament of one of the lamps and hence find the combined resistance of all three lamps in the circuit drawn in (a)(i). Show clearly how you obtain your answers. [7]
Mrs. Murphy must now decide on what cable to purchase. The shop assistant tells her that types of cable are available as shown in the following table.

Type of cable	maximum current in this cable in A	cost per metre in pence
Class 1	3.0	79
Class 2	5.0	99
Class 3	13.0	149

The larger the current a cable can carry, the more expensive it is. Mrs. Murphy naturally wants to keep cost to a minimum.
(iv) What type of cable should Mrs. Murphy buy? [2]
(v) Mrs. Murphy notices that the conductor of each cable is made of copper, but the cables themselves are all of a different thickness.
Which one of the three types of cable is thickest? [1]

(b) Pat carried out an investigation on the current flowing through a torch bulb when different voltages are applied across its end. She obtains the following results.
(i) Plot the graph of *V* (y-axis) against *I* (x-axis) on graph paper. [3]
(ii) Find the resistance of the filament when the current is 0.09 A.
Show clearly how you obtain your answer. [2]

Voltage *V* in volts	0.50	1.00	2.00	3.00	4.00
Current *I* in amperes	0.07	0.10	0.14	0.17	0.20

(iii) The resistance of this filament changes as the current through it changes.
This is because the temperature of the filament is not constant.
Sketch a voltage-current graph for a metallic conductor at constant temperature. [2]
(NICCEA Sp)

15.
(HF)

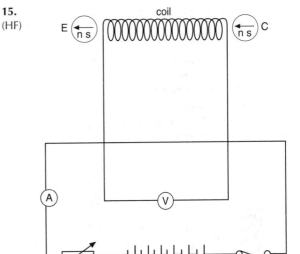

C and E are plotting compasses placed near a 6 Ω coil of wire.

(a) When the switch is closed a current flows in the circuit, **E** and **C** point in the directions shown and the ammeter **A** reads 1.5 A.
(i) Is the direction of the circuit current *clockwise* or *anticlockwise*. [1]
(ii) Calculate the reading on the voltmeter. [2]
(iii) State the polarity of the end of the coil near to plotting compass **C**. [1]

(b) If the circuit resistance is reduced, state the effect, if any, that this would have on
(i) the reading on the ammeter. [1]
(ii) the reading on the voltmeter. [1]
(WJEC Sp)

16.
(HF) **(a)** **(i)** Explain, in terms of electrons, the difference between electrical conductors and insulators. [2]

(ii) A current of 0.5 A flows in a copper wire. Calculate the charge which passes a point on this wire in three seconds. Show clearly how you obtain your answer. [5]

(iii) State the sign of the electric charge moving past the point on the wire. [1]

(b) The diagram below shows the wiring of a 13 A, three pin plug. This plug is used to connect an electric kettle to the ring main circuit.

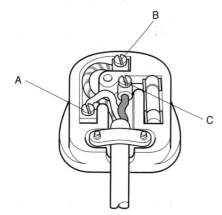

(i) Copy and complete the table below stating the name and colour of the three wires labelled A, B and C. Part of the table has already been completed for you [5]

Wire	Name	Colour
A		
B	Earth	
C		

(ii) Describe and explain the function of wire **B**. [3]

(iii) Many domestic appliances are marked with the symbol ▣ which means they are double insulated and require only two wires. [1]
Which **one** of the three wires listed above is not required? [1]
Explain how double insulation makes this possible. [1]

(c) Northern Ireland Electricity plc charges 7.87 pence for a unit of electricity. Last quarter Mrs. McKibbin was charged £94.44 for the units consumed.

(i) How many units did Mrs. McKibbin use last quarter?
Show clearly how you obtain your answer. [2]

(ii) The 'unit' which appears on a electricity bill is the quantity of energy used by a 1 kW fire in 1 hour. The unit is called a kilowatt hour (kWh). Find the number of joules in a kWh.
Show clearly how you obtain your answer. [2]

(iii) Using your answer to **(c)(ii)** find how many megajoules (MJ) of electrical energy Mrs. McKibbin used in the last three months.
Show clearly how you obtain your answer. [3]

(d) The graph below shows how the resistance of a metal wire changes with length. The wire has a cross section area of 1 mm².

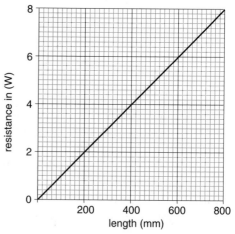

(i) Use the information from the graph to calculate the resistivity of the metal in Ω mm. Show clearly how you obtain your answer. [5]
(NICCEA Sp)

17. The first diagram shows a model head wearing a wig.
(HF) The model is earthed.
The second shows the same model and wig, connected to a + 10 000 V dc supply.
In each diagram the stand holding the head is made from an insulator.

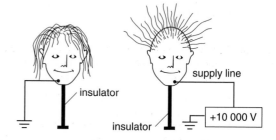

(a) (i) When charged by the +10 000 V dc supply, what type of charge collects on the model? [1]

(ii) In the supply line, do the electrons move *towards* the model or *away* from the model? [1]

(b) Now a –10 000 V dc supply is used instead of the +10 000 V dc supply.
What happens to the electrons and hair this time? [2]
(NEAB Sp)

18. **(a)** Explain, in terms of the motion of molecules, how a
(HG) gas is able to exert a pressure in a sealed container. [3]

(b) A tin-can is being heated. The lid is pressed on firmly so that no air can escape.

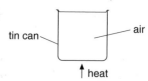

(i) When the tin-can is heated, what happens to
1. the mass of air in the tin-can. [1]
2. the density of the air in the tin-can. [1]

(ii) Explain why the pressure of the air in the tin-can increases when the temperature is increased. [2]
(London Examinations Sp)

19.
(HG)
The diagram below represents a lithium atom of mass number 7.

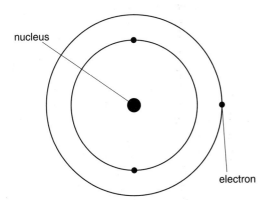

(a) State the atomic number. [1]

(b) State the total number of charged particles in the atom. [1]

(c) State the number of uncharged particles in the nucleus. [1]

(d) Name the positively charged particles in the nucleus. [1]

(e) Explain how the electrons are held in orbit around the nucleus. [1]

(f) This atom may also be represented by ^Y_X Li.

Write down the value of X. [1]
Write down the value of Y. [1]
(WJEC Sp)

20.
(HG)
(a) A radioactive material is thought to emit alpha and gamma radiation. Describe with the help of a diagram, how you could show this is the case. [4]

(b) (i) Explain what is meant by the half-life of a radioactive substance.
(ii) The activity of a radioactive substance was monitored using a geiger-counter. Initially the counter rate was 900 per minute. This fell to 300 per minute after 5 hours. After a day the count rate remained steady at 100 per minute.
1. What was the cause of the steady count rate of 100 per minute?
2. Calculate the half-life of the sample. [4]

(c) State and describe briefly either one medical or one industrial use of radioactivity. [2]
(WJEC Sp)

21.
(HG)
A teacher used the apparatus shown in the diagram to demonstrate radioactivity to a class.

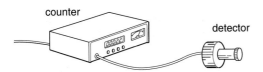

(a) The teacher started the counter then stopped it after one minute. A count of 22 was shown.
Why did the counter show a reading even though no radioactive source was being used. [1]

(b) The teacher then used the detector investigate the types of radiation given off by a radioactive source.

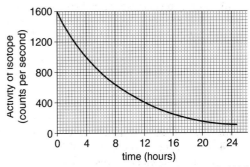

The teacher found the average number of counts per minute with and without absorbers present. The results are shown in the table.

Absorber used	Average counts per minute
No absorber	1 973
Card 1 mm thick	1 216
Lead 1 mm thick	22

State whether or not each of the following radiations is given out by the source. Give your reason for each answer.
(i) Alpha [2]
(ii) Beta [2]
(iii) Gamma [2]

(c) The graph shows how the radioactivity of an isotope of technetium changes with time.

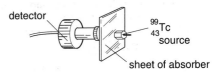

(i) Explain what is meant by the term half life. [2]
(ii) Use the graph to calculate the half life of this isotope. [2]
(NEAB Sp)

22.
(HF)
(a) Satellites are often placed in polar orbit or in geostationary orbit around the Earth. A polar orbit is shown on the diagram.

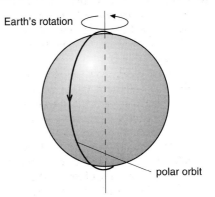

(i) Sketch the diagram above and add a geostationary orbit to it. [1]
(ii) Give ONE use for each type of satellite.
1. Polar orbit satellite [1]
2. Geostationary orbit satellite [1]

The table gives data for a polar and a geostationary satellite.

Satellite	Radius of orbit (km)	Mass (kg)
geostationary	42000	2000
polar	6700	2000

(iii) State the type of force the Earth exerts on each satellite. [1]

(iv) Suggest why the size of the force that the Earth exerts on the two satellites is different. State which force is the smaller. [2]

(v) The mass of the polar orbit satellite is 2000 kg. It is transferred to a geostationary orbit. Its mass is now:

much less than 2000 kg
just less than 2000 kg
2000 kg
much more than 2000 kg

Write out the correct answer. [1]

(b) Microwaves are used to communicate with a polar orbiting satellite. The satellite orbits the Earth once every 90 minutes.

(i) Explain why sound waves cannot be used for satellite communication. [1]

(ii) A ground station cannot receive signals from a polar orbiting satellite at all times. Explain why. [2]

(iii) The distance round the orbit is 42 000 km. Calculate the speed of the satellite in km/h. [3]

(London Examinations Sp)

23. This question is about satellites and space exploration.
(HH) (a) Communication satellites are usually put into an orbit high above the equator called a geostationary orbit.

(i) Explain what is meant by a geostationary orbit. [1]

(ii) What is the advantage of such an orbit for communicating from one part of the world to another. [1]

(iii) What is the time for a complete orbit of this satellite? [1]

(iv) Why must it be placed at a particular height above the Earth's surface? [1]

(v) Why is the orbit above the equator? [1]

(b) Write a full account of how a star changes over a long period of time. [5]

(WJEC Sp)

INDEX

If a reference is given in **bold**, you should look that up first